Socialize Your Patient Engagement Strategy

Socialize Your Patient Engagement Strategy makes the case for a fundamentally new approach to healthcare communication; one that mobilizes patients, healthcare professionals and uses new media to enable gathering, sharing and communication of information to achieve patient-centricity and provide better value for both organizations and patients.

Letitia Affinito and John Mack focus on three priority areas for actions: Improving Health Literacy (web sites; targeted mass digital campaigns), Improving Self-care (self-management education; self-monitoring; self-treatment), Improving Patient Safety (adherence to treatment regimens; equipping patients for safer selfcare).

The authors explain the healthcare context to the digital communications revolution; the emerging digital marketing and communications techniques that enable this revolution and the core elements behind a patient-driven digital strategy.

Drawing on their research and consulting practices; the practical experience of managers in medium-large companies worldwide; interviews with experts and leading case histories, the book provides a proven framework for improving the development and implementation of patient-centered digital communication programs in healthcare organizations.

Effective patient-centric communication crosses all organizational boundaries. Putting the patient first is a priority for ALL healthcare communicators and here is the book to enable you to do just that.

To my husband, Alessandro, my son, Leonardo, and to those of you who are committed to doing good while doing well.
Letizia Affinito

To my wife, Debbie, whose hard work and support makes it possible for me to be PharmaGuy. I am lucky to be HerGuy.
John Mack

Socialize Your Patient Engagement Strategy

How Social Media and Mobile Apps Can Boost Health Outcomes

LETIZIA AFFINITO
Adjunct Professor of Marketing Communications
Founder and CEO of Brandnew MC

and

JOHN MACK (aka Pharmaguy)
Pharma Marketing Pundit,
Publisher of Pharma Marketing News *and Pharma*
Marketing Blog

Taking an active part to the changing game of health management to improve people's health while getting a greater value for your organization.

Routledge
Taylor & Francis Group

LONDON AND NEW YORK

First published in paperback 2024

First published 2015 by Gower Publishing

Published 2016 by Routledge
4 Park Square, Milton Park, Abingdon, Oxon OX14 4RN

and by Routledge
605 Third Avenue, New York, NY 10158

Routledge is an imprint of the Taylor & Francis Group, an informa business

British Library Cataloguing in Publication Data
A catalogue record for this book is available from the British Library

The Library of Congress has cataloged the printed edition as follows:
Affinito, Letizia, author.
  Socialize your patient engagement strategy : how social media and mobile apps can boost health outcomes / by Letizia Affinito and John Mack.
     p. ; cm.
  Includes bibliographical references and index.
  ISBN 978-1-4724-5632-8 (hardback)
  I. Mack, John, 1947- , author. II. Title.
  [DNLM: 1. Marketing of Health Services. 2. Professional-Patient Relations.
  3. Communication. 4. Delivery of Health Care. 5. Mobile Applications. 6. Social Media.
W 74.1]
  RA410.56
  610.68'8--dc23
                                                                    2015010836

  ISBN: 978-1-4724-5632-8 (hbk)
  ISBN: 978-1-03-283726-0 (pbk)
  ISBN: 978-1-315-60971-3 (ebk)

  DOI: 10.4324/9781315609713

Contents

List of Figures

List of Tables

About the Authors

Letizia Affinito—Founder and CEO of Brandnew MC—has worked for over 20 years in Strategic Marketing Communications both as manager and consultant. She advises several multinational companies and organizations on online/offline communication strategy matters.

Letizia has a PhD in Management and teaches as Adjunct Professor at leading International Universities and Business Schools. Her education includes the Case Method Teaching Seminar (Part I and II), the Executive Program in Digital Marketing at Harvard Business School, and the Young Managers Executive Programme at INSEAD.

In 2012, Affinito launched *Web in Salute*, the first online research project in Italy exploring the "Effects of Online Health Information Seeking on Physician/Patient's Actions". It is an independent project that employs a survey of a national sample of consumers, pharmacists, and HCPs to gain insights about actual health care experiences and outcomes, rather than opinions and attitudes as a result of online health information seeking.

Prior to founding Brandnew Marketing Communications, Affinito worked at Serono where she was responsible for marketing and sales activities in the Endocrinology and Metabolism Business Unit. While at Serono she was featured in a "success story" that was included in the global company magazine *Paradigm*.

Previously, Affinito worked as a manager for Burson Marsteller in Rome where she was responsible for business development, strategic communication, media relations, activities/tactics implementation and budget management and control.

Prior to that, she was a product manager for Merck Sharp & Dohme where, also as a member of the European Management Development Team, she was responsible for marketing and sales activities of the antibiotic TIENAM (Hospital Business) in Rome, Italy.

John Mack—known as "PharmaGuy" on Twitter and in drug industry circles—is a thought leader in pharmaceutical marketing with more than 30 years experience in the digital space, including interactive game design, computer-based learning, drug website development, e-health ethics, and social media.

In 1995, Mack created PharmInfoNet, an award-winning drug information Web site, which was later sold to Mediconsult.com—a health portal site for consumers and physicians. After selling PharmInfoNet to Mediconsult.com Mack became the company's Director of Drug Information Services.

Later, as a consultant with AnswerThink—a digital agency—Mack helped develop and launch several drug.com and medical society websites. One consulting project involved the creation of an e-business charter for a major pharmaceutical company. Mack also helped several pharmaceutical companies develop privacy/HIPAA internal guidelines for marketing & sales.

In 1997, Mack co-founded and headed the Internet Healthcare Coalition, a non-profit 301(c) organization dedicated to improving the quality and reliability of health information on the Internet. The Coalition published the e-Health Code of Ethics in 1999.

Currently, Mack is the publisher of *Pharma Marketing News*—an independent monthly electronic newsletter focused on issues of importance to pharmaceutical marketing executives. It is a service of the Pharma Marketing Network—The First Forum for Pharmaceutical Marketing Experts—which brings together pharmaceutical marketing professionals from manufacturers, communications companies, and marketing service providers for wide ranging discussions and education on a multitude of current topics.

Mack is known as PharmaGuy (@pharmaguy) on Twitter and other social media sites and is the author of the award-winning Pharma Marketing Blog, which was cited by the *Wall Street Journal* as "A 'Must Read' Blog for Insiders." Each year PharmaGuy presents the PharmaGuy Social Media/Mobile Pioneer Award to a deserving pharma marketing team or person. The Award recognizes marketing and other communication campaigns that have "pioneered" the use of social media and/or mobile platforms for the delivery of innovative marketing, corporate communications, patient support, and disease awareness programs.

Mack has a B.A. degree (chemistry major) from Franklin & Marshall College, M.S. and MPhil degrees in biochemistry from Columbia University, and an M.A. degree in communication arts & computer graphics from the New York Institute of Technology.

Acknowledgments

Saying this book is "by Letizia Affinito" is overstated. Without the significant contributions made by other people, this book would certainly not exist. At the top of the list is John Mack who accepted to contribute when I asked him and accompanied me on this exciting journey from the first raw idea to the final work. I had been following John (aka Pharmaguy) through his Pharma Marketing Blog and *Pharma Marketing News* since my first approach to pharma digital marketing in 2007. We had never met before and he trusted me right away in embarking on this challenging writing adventure. We both knew how demanding the topic was and the difficulties we could have encountered but we got to the end and I realized a long-lasting dream united by a shared goal: contribute to make patient-centered digital communication a reality. I was truly blessed to have an extraordinary partner trusting me and dedicated to the project. I am indebted to him and a few other critical readers for investing hours in their reading drafts of the manuscript and feeding me the brutal facts about what needed to be improved.

I would like to give a special thanks to a number of executives from many different health organizations who were willing to share their case histories. Especially, I would like to thank Gabriel Eicher, General Manager, PatientsLikeMe; Amy Burnett Heldman, MPH—Communications Lead, CDC Division for Heart Disease and Stroke Prevention CDC; Trish Nettleship, Global Director Social Media and Influence, UCB, and Paul G. Matsen, Chief Marketing and Communications Officer, Cleveland Clinic for patiently reviewing my contents and giving their insights and comments.

I owe a lot to Fard Johnmar, Founder and President of Enspektos, John M. McKeever, Executive Vice President of Gelb Consulting, Michalis A. Michael, CEO at DigitalMR, McKinsey, and Forrest Research for sharing their contents and charts.

I would like to make a special note of Jonathan Norman as my publisher at Gower Publishing who has enthusiastically believed in and supported this book from the moment he received my proposal.

Finally, I am profoundly thankful for my immense good luck to have a lovely family and many old friends who tolerate my "dynamic" nature and tendency to get enthusiastic with projects such as this one. I would like to thank each of them for not letting me down while I was busy over the last few years and making me feel their closeness every time it was needed.

Letizia Affinito

Foreword

There is no one to help you or to bind up your injury. No medicine can heal you.

New Living Translation, Jeremiah 30:13.

The dilemma of biblical times and past centuries was not merely a lack of patient engagement as much as traditional healing had little to offer the disease-ridden population. The cognitive tasks involved in diagnosis were largely limited to what was observable and what little was able to be described by the patient.

Rene Theophile Hyacinthe Laënnec (1781–1826), a French physician, invented the stethoscope in 1816 and the world would never be the same for the medical establishment. Ironically, the development of the stethoscope, a true technological marvel that allowed the doctor to hear the inner workings of the patient, may actually be more responsible for contributing to a lack of a patient-centered communications approach than any other medical advancement. For while patient-centered communication (or more precisely, the act of facilitating behavior) enables patients to express their perspective on illness, treatment, and other health-related behaviors, the absence of engagement and of inhibiting behavior typically discourages a patient's collaboration.

In his original article published in 2007 in *The Journal of Ethics*, "Technology and the Patient-Physician Relationship: A Defining Historic Moment," Stanley J. Reiser, MD, MPA, PhD, current Griff T. Ross Professor of Humanities and Technology in Health Care at The University of Texas Health Science Center at Houston, and also Associate Director of The John P. McGovern, M.D. Center for Health, Humanities, and the Human Spirit, wrote the following of Laënnec's stethoscope:

> *[His] simple technology gave physicians a new set of accurate signs of disease that increased the precision of their diagnoses, but it had the unforeseen consequence of altering their relationship with patients. Why seek to inquire into the lives of patients to gain insights into their illness, which not only took time but was fraught with undependability stemming from forgetfulness, exaggeration, embarrassment and other*

contingencies that introduced error into their account, if a technique
existed that gave doctors the ability to locate and evaluate significant
signs of disease by themselves? The stethoscope and the technique
of auscultation it furthered created a paradigm of examination that
continues to be a major force in the medicine of today.

Oliver Wendell Holmes, MD (1809–1894), one of America's best-known
medical and literary figures of the nineteenth century, studied in Paris from
1833 to 1835 with Pierce C. A. Louis, a former student of Laënnec. After a brief
stint addressing the needs of patients in his clinical practice, Holmes turned to
academic medicine, ultimately serving at Harvard Medical School as Professor
of Anatomy and Physiology from 1847 to 1882 and later as Dean from 1847 to
1853. Although most of his literary work was not medically-oriented, nearly
two decades following the discovery of the stethoscope, Holmes wrote a
somewhat satirical piece in 1848 named the "The Stethoscope Song." At the
end of the piece, he writes,

> *Now use your ears, all you that can,*
> *But don't forget to mind your eyes,*
> *Or you may be cheated, like this young man,*
> *By a couple of silly, abnormal flies.*

"As we listen, there is much to be learned from our powers of observation and
touch as well. Holmes's poem also cautions the user of new technology to be
aware of its limitations. So while we are amused and entertained by Holmes's
humor and satire, we should not fail to take heed of his more subtle messages,"
wrote Robert J. Hall, MD, Emeritus Director, Cardiology Education, Texas
Heart Institute and St. Luke's Episcopal Hospital and Former Editor, *Texas
Heart Institute Journal* in his original article published in 2005 in the *Texas Heart
Institute Journal*. This tenet—multiple paths should be simultaneously accessed
to communicate with the body of the patient—can easily be expanded to
the broader physician–patient relationship itself, where multiple avenues of
communication used concurrently can help both the medical professional and
the patient understand each other's ideas, concerns, and queries to optimize
medical care.

In her original article published in 2001 in the *British Medical Journal* in
support of an "emerging international definition of patient-centered care,"
Moira Stewart, PhD, Professor, current Distinguished University Professor
at the Centre for Studies in Family Medicine at Western University and the

Dr. Brian W. Gilbert Canada Research Chair in Primary Health Care Research, and colleagues wrote:

> *Patients want patient-centered care which (a) explores the patients'*
> *main reason for the visit, concerns, and need for information; (b) seeks*
> *an integrated understanding of the patients' world—that is, their whole*
> *person, emotional needs, and life issues; (c) finds common ground on*
> *what the problem is and mutually agrees on management; (d) enhances*
> *prevention and health promotion; and (e) enhances the continuing*
> *relationship between the patient and the doctor.*

While recognized and endorsed by many as the preferred method of communication and engagement, a patient-centered approach (whether they are digital immigrants or natives) means that for patients we must participate in a dialogue that conveys medical and therapeutic information and instructions about which approaches to care that may serve best. Ideally, patient-centered interactions take into account the individual's particular circumstance, concerns, cultural differences, health literacy levels, language differences, personal preferences, and socioeconomic status. Engagement must occur in real-time—they now expect every interaction to happen swiftly and seamlessly.

For clinicians, a patient-centered approach means equipping them to provide value—evidence-based information about questions they may face daily in their virtual or in-depth clinical environment and preparing them to actively engage the patients' ideas, expectations, and feelings regarding illness, and addressing their psychosocial context. The clinician's probing communication and active listening skills are interdependent and crucial to the patient-centered approach—a bold departure from the institutionalized (and outdated) parochial and paternalistic, detached approach to patient care. For success to occur, clinicians will need to be nimble and adaptive to the language and style of patients now engaged in a digital world. While it does not necessarily mean changing the meaning of what may be important for the patient, it does involve moving in direct parallel to the ever-changing needs or the patient and understanding/addressing the requirement for increased, random access across digital channels (in addition to the live engagement in close confines of the examination room). With the pace of patient-centered digital communications increasing exponentially as the technology involves (indeed, it almost warrants the need to develop a Turing test for predicting patient–physician engagement!), clinicians increasingly realize that they have little time to address the changes in their practice. Adopting new digital technologies may ultimately help reinforce patients' confidence in their ability to co-manage their own disease, leading to improvements in both adherence and compliance with treatment regimens and in turn improve their overall health.

For researchers, it means that, in addition to the funding of patient-centered comparative clinical effectiveness research through groups, like the non-profit, non-governmental organization, Patient-Centered Outcomes Research Institute (PCORI), we need to explore how we can improve patient understanding and improve on how they can initially act and continuously comply with digital health information. Is it a crisis of understanding medical information? Is it a problem of access to information? In its most basic form, researchers can help ensure and validate that the best language is selected and the methods and materials that are adopted or adapted for use by clinicians in their digital dialogue with patients. In its most advanced form, research can conduct the critical evaluation of online content and assess the outcomes of further engaging and empowering the digitally-savvy patient in a patient-centered approach.

For companies focused on the life sciences, it reinforces the need for these individuals and institutions to become stewards of this dynamic series of relationships and the need to deliver a meaningful and consistent engagement across all stakeholders. The end customer the companies serve needs to be heavily involved. The company may need to create a new approach to support each stakeholder's unique experience—adopt a continuous test and learn approach, while listening to the evolving needs for immediacy and convenience, and integrating the latest digital, mobile, and social technologies. With the rate of diffusion accelerating, many companies need to go beyond just keeping pace or they will be outpaced—moving quickly isn't always the easiest to navigate but prioritization needs to be given to the migrating to a new digital process to address the adoption rates of digital resources that clinicians and patients will be using to support their decision-making. There are questions about treatments and as both clinicians and patients become more digitally empowered and engaged, each will be seeking support while exchanging their ideas, experiences, and thoughts with each other and across the communities they participate in on social media and in their daily interactions. How can the company and brand help contribute to this experience? What is the pathway for the patient-centered digital communications journey? Although the questions are not easily answered, they must be addressed boldly nonetheless, and the path that their answers chart must be fully explored.

Much like a stethoscope metaphor, the contents herein will enhance the reader's ability to listen to the unmet needs of patients, support the design and development of digital strategies and solutions, and ultimately help achieve remarkable value regardless of whether the reader is a newcomer or a senior colleague who expertly speaks the language of all stakeholders. For the patient, healthcare practitioner, academic scholar, or industry curator sometime in the future that is searching for relevancy in your work today, my personal hope is that the engaging with an empowered patient as a partner is now the underpinning of all healthcare communications. This book comprehensively defines the current environment in 2015 and clearly articulates how to integrate effective patient-engagement digital strategies into the market communications mix. My hope is that our analytics and insights work will have moved the path forward to a time of co-creation with the patients' voices and needs at the heart of every communication. The mark of success for these efforts will be a time in the future where the mere title of this tome will be synonymous with improved health outcomes. As we strive to move communications forward and continue to make advances in digital, mobile, and social technologies, we will be better equipped to support and enable patients to live the best possible quality of life with their disease or condition.

Mario R. Nacinovich, Jr. MSc,
Managing Partner, AXON and
Editor emeritus, *Journal of Communication in Healthcare*

Preface

My first approach to health marketing communication dates back to 1993 while taking my CSS Programme at Harvard. At that time a "new" trend was starting in the health industry: communicating to the patient!

More than 20 years have passed and I am witnessing a "new" trend in the health industry: the rise of the empowered patient!

"Patient Centricity" is becoming more and more important for successful health organizations. Nevertheless, we can still count on one hand the few organizations committed to it.

In addition, while access to information has improved, health communication managers have little time to review, select, and read all the materials providing insights and tools on this important topic.

After researching for more than seven years, I decided to write a book about patient-centered digital communication strategy to provide the basic information and tools needed by health communication managers who wish to use new technology in their relations with patients.

I would love to hear from readers about what works for them and what doesn't. I view this book as a starting point of a constructive exchange of ideas that hopefully will help make patient-centered digital communication a reality.

I hope you will find value in these pages and will enjoy the journey as much as I did in writing it with my friend John Mack, also known as Pharmaguy.

Letizia Affinito
laffinito@brandnewmc.com
Rome, Italy

Introduction

Worldwide healthcare is in crisis. Healthcare systems are struggling with raising costs and unequal quality. None of the solutions (that is, attacking fraud, reducing errors, enforcing practice guidelines, making patients better "consumers," implementing electronic medical records or EMRs) tried so far by healthcare leaders and policy makers have had much impact. It's time to put maximization of value for patients at the core of the strategy: that is, achieving the best outcomes at the lowest cost.[1]

As Michael E. Porter and Thomas H. Lee say:

> We must move away from a supply-driven health care system organized around what physicians do and toward a patient-centered system organized around what patients need. We must shift the focus from the volume and profitability of services provided—physician visits, hospitalizations, procedures, and tests—to the patient outcomes achieved. This transformation must come from within. Only physicians and provider organizations can put in place the set of interdependent steps needed to improve value, because ultimately value is determined by how medicine is practiced. Yet every other stakeholder in the health care system has a role to play. Patients, health plans, employers, and suppliers (including pharmaceutical and biomedical companies) can hasten the transformation—and all will benefit greatly from doing so.

A Digital Health Communication Strategy designed around the patient can play a major role in driving the needed transformation.

Indeed, throughout the many years of our combined experience in the health sector, we have witnessed the changing role of the patient. Recently, we have heard the word "patient-centered" mentioned thousands of times by health communicators, but we can count just a small number of projects and programs that really put the patient at the center of their strategy and focus. Being user-centered is the strategy that will support the business in the long term.

Let's take, for example, the pharmaceutical organizations' patent model and subsequent relationship with healthcare providers. It has always followed traditional models of consumerism: "we are a drug company and we've produced this drug which you can buy from us." So, one must be wondering, how can health communicators working in pharma support and facilitate patients' desires for greater inclusion and authority in their care and still turn a profit?

Firstly, they need to reshape their relationship with the people they serve. Pharmaceutical companies can no longer act as vendors and must become partners to professionals and patients alike. In doing so, they need to provide solutions, not just pills, and increasingly this will mean delivering holistic services and systems of care. "Beyond the pill" solutions are an arena in which there is massive potential for pharmaceutical companies to add real value.

While there are books that focus on specific healthcare communicators within different types of organizations, in our book we recognize that effective patient-centric communication crosses all organizational boundaries. That is, putting the patient first is a priority for ALL healthcare communicators and our book focuses on how to achieve that and provide better value for both organizations (in terms of profit) and patients (in terms of better service and improved health). Consumers have long used health websites and other online tools to gather information about conditions and treatments. Now they are broadening their health activity online, using Internet resources to support healthcare decision-making and to manage conditions, a new study shows.

Forty-five percent of online US adults with a chronic condition say that the Internet is essential to managing their disease or condition, according to the Cybercitizen Health® US 2013 study from healthcare market research and advisory firm Manhattan Research.[2]

The study also found that online content and services influence how consumers approach health management for themselves and their dependents, with 44 percent of online consumers agreeing that the Internet is essential for their health and medical decision-making.

These and other study findings highlight key opportunities for various health stakeholders, such as pharmaceutical companies, provider networks, physicians organizations, patients associations, and payers, to provide technology-based value-added services and empower deeper engagement from end users.

While the Internet provides practically unlimited potential for acquiring new knowledge, rash, unconsidered acceptance of its content can mislead. Therefore, one cannot be considered digitally literate until he/she has the ability to judge the reliability of online information.[3] Unfortunately, critical evaluation of online information is generally lacking in society.

In addition, with the recession and healthcare legislation driving the focus on saving money, Medicare and other payers are looking to cut costs. Prevention, hospital stay reduction, post-treatment visits reduction, side effects prevention, and clinic risk reduction are only some of the priorities to save costs for payers while improving the health of people/patients.

As an example, getting people to take their medicine correctly cuts costs for hospitals, creates revenue for pharmaceutical companies, and improves patient health. But changing healthcare habits will require better, more effective communication by insurers, healthcare equipment and services organizations, pharmaceuticals, biotechnology, and related life sciences companies focused on preventative and wellness care. Keeping up with digital technology and social media communication channels used by patients is crucial.

The situation is ripe for change.

Indeed, digital marketing is relatively new in all industries, including healthcare. Executives have consequently realized their need to have a digital strategy in place as a part of their larger marketing strategy.

The role of social media in healthcare and its impact on patient engagement is moving to center stage, propelled by mobile technology, patient demand, and growing influence of the digital native generation. However, for the most part, the healthcare sector is not yet ready for these empowered and digitally demanding patients.

As of today, digital marketing is not largely distinguishable from traditional marketing. Companies tend to split marketing practices into different components such as digital or multichannel, but the real changes are the strategy behind the introduction of the new available digital tools. The structure within pharmaceutical companies' marketing teams, for example, has largely remained the same. The same can be said for their targets' structures, including physicians, payers, patients, and pharmacists.

Advancing social media to center stage in health communication will require clarity from regulators, a more proactive stance by pharmaceutical manufacturers to engage with patients, and utilization of available tools to ensure patients receive value from their social media interactions.

The healthcare industry has a unique opportunity to use Internet and social media tools to provide better value for both organizations (in terms of profit) and for patients (in terms of better service and improved health). By reading this book, you are taking a step forward to seize that opportunity.

What You Will Learn From This Book

The constantly evolving digital world must be used in the practice of medicine to improve the care of patients. However, the only way to do so effectively is via evidence-based, meaningful and strategic use. *Socialize Your Patient Engagement Strategy* provides practical guidance in this mission and is thus essential reading for all health stakeholders looking into approaching this for the first time.

Drawing on the authors' research and consulting practice, as well as on the practical experience of managers in medium–large companies worldwide, the book will provide critical insights for developing and implementing a patient-centered digital health communication program within your organization. You'll discover how major health companies have leveraged major social media platforms such as LinkedIn, Facebook, YouTube, Twitter, Pinterest, Tumblr, blogs, and mobile apps to deliver their messages and valuable health solutions to the growing "e-patient" audience. We will offer tips, advice, and critical reviews that every stakeholder in the healthcare system will find useful in developing a patient-centric communication program designed to *improve their ability to engage with empowered patients and thereby improve health outcomes.*

In particular, the book will highlight four priority areas for actions (or levers):

1. *Improving health literacy (for example, websites and targeted mass digital campaigns):* The starting point to transform social media into a useful patient empowerment tool is to unleash the health literacy-driven power of the patient. Companies that push the

responsibility for doing this to the widest and lowest possible levels in the organization will be the successful ones.

2.   *Improving self-care (for example, self-management education, self-monitoring, and self-treatment)*: Behind the democratic view of a patient-centered health system lies a significant focus and investment in disease-management education, disease monitoring, and treatment tools and training. Indeed, companies can re-ignite and nurture the patients' self-care abilities by developing valuable tools and delivering tailor-made training programs.

3.   *Improving patient safety (for example, adherence to treatment regimens and equipping patients for safer self-care)*: The role patients can play in improving the safety of their care has been recognized only recently, and research into this issue is still in its early stages. Nevertheless, successful partnerships with patients to reduce errors and improve safety can only occur in environments where patient involvement is valued and supported. Issues of health literacy must also be tackled before information about safety and risk can be effectively communicated to patients and acted upon by them.

What You Will Find in This Book

We have structured the book into three sections. The first section presents an overview of the current situation and the main basic concepts and regulations you need to learn before embarking on a digital health communication program. The second provides some useful tools to understand the marketplace and consumers in order to design and implement a successful patient-centered digital strategy as examined in the third section. These three parts comprise ten chapters:

Chapter 1: *Creating and Capturing Patient Value* introduces the basic concepts of digital health marketing communication. In it, after discussing the leading trends and forces affecting health marketing communication in this era of social media and patient empowerment, I discuss the key steps in the digital communication process and introduce the topic of value creation with a case history from the Cleveland Clinic (CC). (Letizia Affinito)

Chapter 2: *Digital Health Content Regulations, Guidelines and Ethics* lays out the basic premise that, with patients needing and accessing information throughout their journey, the relevance and quality of information needs to be ensured. Quality of information is, in fact, becoming a greater concern, which also serves as a driver of positive change for online information sources and calls to action from individuals who are eager to share their information and knowledge.

In this chapter I include updated guidelines for reliable digital health and online health information. (John Mack)

Chapter 3: *Listening to Patients Can Fuel More Personalized Communication* explains how to use the rise of online conversations for research purposes with tools such as private online communities and active/passive web listening. I introduce this critical topic analyzing a case study from UCB and a number of other significant examples from the healthcare industry. We'll see how passive listening can be far more action-oriented and intent-filled than it sounds. (Letizia Affinito)

Chapter 4: *The Emergence of Online Opinion Leaders* explores how to accurately identify and manage digital key opinion leaders (KOLs) (for example, online physicians, institution representatives, and patients) to successfully promote health communication initiatives and projects.

In fact, the number of factors influencing physician prescribing decisions and their communication with patients continues to grow, including clinical experience, journal articles, continuing medical education (CME) activity, managed care, detailing, events, journal advertising, patient requests, online information seeking, and so on. However, one of the most impactful influences on physicians has remained consistent: national, regional and/or local KOLs. I will present a leading case history on "Collaborating with Online Physician Communities Pharma-Physician Peer-to-Peer Dialog via Sermo." (John Mack)

Chapter 5: *Building a Winning Digital Communication Strategy for Patients* gives a quick overview of key customer-driven marketing communication strategy decisions—dividing markets into meaningful customer groups (segmentation), choosing which customer groups to serve (targeting), creating communication initiatives and tools which best serve targeted customers (differentiation), and positioning them in the mind of patients (positioning). It introduces a key analysis tool from Forrester Research (2013), the Social Technographics Score, a new model which focuses on commercial social behaviors, which, differently from many other surveys, is based on how audiences interact with and talk about companies, brands, and products. (Letizia Affinito)

Chapter 6: *Developing an Integrated Marketing Communication Strategy* looks further into how all communication must be planned and blended into carefully integrated programs to deliver a clear, consistent, and compelling message about its organization and its brands. I'll do it starting from a successful national initiative, Million Hearts©, launched by the Department of Health and Human Services (HHS) in September 2011, which has set an ambitious goal to prevent one million heart attacks and strokes by 2017. (Letizia Affinito)

Chapter 7: *Integrating Digital into Your Marketing Communication Mix* takes a deeper look at the digital marketing mix: the tactical tools and actions that managers use to implement their strategies and develop superior customer/patient value such as:

- developing compelling content;

- developing apps that meet patients', physicians' and healthcare needs;

- developing and managing advocacy programs;

- developing and igniting online virality.

We'll present a successfully integrated mobile app ad campaign from Astellas. (Letizia Affinito and John Mack)

Chapter 8: *Digital Patient Storytelling and Peer-Influenced Marketing* shows how health organizations use Point of View (POV) marketing to connect to their customers and patients more effectively.

POV is a technique used in film to create emphasis for a storyline. Changes in visual and verbal aspects of the film help the audience quickly and collectively create expectations of the storyline. Brands which can base some of their marketing communication on POV are able to connect their brands' audience in a way traditional marketing fails to. I demonstrate with a case study from Janssen Therapeutics, the *PREZISTA Zone*. (John Mack)

Chapter 9: *Measuring the Results of Your Digital Efforts* explores some new approaches to analyzing healthcare digital campaigns results. I start by exploring some of the main ways to measure the success of digital communication with examples from Cleveland Clinic and other healthcare organizations. (Letizia Affinito)

Chapter 10: *Crowdsourcing and Co-creating for a Patient-Centered Health Communication* introduces and explains crowdsourcing and co-creation, how they differ, and how they can represent a very effective way to encourage communication among patients and between patients and health providers (both physicians and pharma/biomedical managers). We'll also see, through a number of examples, that, if well planned and implemented, a crowdsourcing or co-creation project can become an "innovative" way to engage patients and generate change while communicating a message (that is, disease prevention) or a brand. I'll begin with a leading case history about crowdsourcing in action at PatientsLikeMe. (Letizia Affinito)

Notes

1   Porter, M.E. and Lee, T.H. (2013), The Strategy That Will Fix Health Care, *Harvard Business Review*, 91, no. 10 (October 2013):50–70.
2   Manhattan Research. (2013), Digital tools and online health services poised to play key role in consumer health management, study finds. [online] Available at http://manhattanresearch.com/News-and-Events/Press-Releases/consumer-health-management [Accessed April 11 2015].
3   Gilster, P. (1997), *A Primer on Digital Literacy*. Mississauga, Ontario: John Wiley & Sons; Ivanitskaya, L., O'Boyle, I. and Casey, A.M. (2006), Health Information Literacy and Competencies of Information Age Students; Results from the Interactive Online Research Readiness Self-Assessment (RRSA), *Journal of Medical Internet Research*, 8(2):e6; Norman, C.D. and Skinner, H.A. (2006), eHealth Literacy: Essential Skills for Consumer Health in a Networked World, *Journal of Medical Internet Research*, 8(2):e9.

PART I
Approaching Digital Health Communication

Chapter 1

Creating and Capturing Patient Value

LETIZIA AFFINITO

 Developing an effective patient-centered digital strategy is one of the biggest challenges in today's evolving healthcare industry. Starting off on the right foot, for health communication managers, either from healthcare equipment and services organizations or pharmaceuticals, biotechnology and related life sciences companies, requires having a clear understanding of some basic concepts which will help them go through the Digital Health Communication Strategy Process to create and capture patient value.

In this chapter we introduce the basic concepts of digital health communication. After discussing the leading trends and forces affecting health communication in this era of social media and patient engagement, we start by defining digital health communication and then discuss the key steps in the digital communication process—from monitoring patient discussions on the web (primarily social media) to understanding patient needs, designing patient-driven health digital strategies and integrated communication programs, building patient relationships, and, finally, creating patient value.

We'll begin our journey with a leading case history on digital communication in action at Cleveland Clinic (CC), the first major academic medical center to make patient experience a strategic goal, the first to appoint a Chief Experience Officer, and one of the first academic medical centers to establish an Office of

Patient Experience. The secret to CC's success is its commitment to the "Patients First" guiding principle. CC has a profound passion for creating patient value and relationships through a patient-centered approach. In return, patients reward CC with advocacy, marketing insights, and loyalty.

Cleveland Clinic: Passionate about Creating Patient Value and Relationships

In thinking about patient-centered healthcare, you cannot avoid thinking first of CC. As a groundbreaker of the patient experience as a strategic goal, it was established in 1921 for the purpose of providing patient care, research, and medical education.[1]

In 2004, CC designed and implemented the "Patient First" program to focus more deeply on the well-being of its patients. Making the stay at CC "a nice experience" became a central goal. This included the introduction of the new title and role of Chief Experience Officer. Among other reasons, the move stemmed from understanding that an attention to emotional well-being, along with education, compliance, and patient engagement, actually contributed to the success of the entire cycle. The mindset of service opened CC employees to identify issues such as patient anxiety, dissatisfaction with food, missed appointments, and long waits on the phone—all of which could affect the outcome of patient conditions. Eliminating these lapses represented gains in patient satisfaction as well as increased efficiency.

One key to the success of the "Patient First" program is CC's effort to improve the online experience and engage patients through its website. The biggest part of this effort is the eClevelandClinic services, which includes MyChart, an EMR. Through the medical record, the patient can receive all their test results and information they need about their recent visit with the physician. Patients not yet signed up for MyChart can go to the clevelandclinic.org website and smoothly make online appointment requests and ask questions.

To create an engaging online experience, CC invested the time of employees who are knowledgeable about the Clinic's brand and its communication key messages. They started by looking at other industries' best benchmarks and at what other healthcare players were doing. Next, they did their own research before setting up a social media council involving people across the health system—from regional hospitals, from legal to HR, from clinical to marketing and communication (cross-functional team). As a result, they set up a social

One key to the success of the "Patient First" program is CC's effort to improve the online experience and engage patients through its website.

media policy to govern employees' behavior in interacting with social media and built a team dedicated to interacting with followers on Facebook and Twitter to make sure patients get quick responses to questions and comments on the two channels. "We track awareness on a quarterly basis," says CC Chief Communications and Marketing Officer, Paul G. Matsen. According to the results of its internal surveys, social media now represents almost 5 percent of awareness of CC.

In one of his most recent interviews,[2] Matsen said:

> About six years ago we were at 15-million visits to clevelandclinic.org. This year we'll finish above 90-million. And one of the things that I stress is that mobile has been transforming the Owned digital media space in the past three to five years, and this is going to continue ... In August, 69 percent of the visits to our website were made on a smartphone or tablet device. Mobile, combined with social media have really been driving tremendous growth on our website. The growth of mobile is highly significant. So having a great mobile user experience is vital, build that into your planning, and think about responsive design. Even when you're thinking about your search campaign, consider if they work on mobile devices. A lot of that is driven by the success we've had in social media. Many people that access their Facebook and other social media accounts do so on their mobile devices, multiple times each day. If you're creating great content, you can pull them through to your website. So, if you haven't designed for mobile from the start you are missing out on a huge part of audience.

Successful organizations providing products and services in the healthcare industry have one thing in common: just like CC, they are extremely patient-centered and greatly committed to communication both internally and externally.

These companies share a commitment to understanding and satisfying patient needs in well-defined target markets. They encourage everyone in the organization to help develop lasting patient relationships based on creating value.

Successful organizations providing products and services in the healthcare industry have one thing in common: just like CC, they are extremely patient-centered and greatly committed to communication both internally and externally.

Today's patients are making health decisions more carefully and reassessing their relationship with brands, being it a drug, healthcare provider, or even a doctor. It's more important than ever to build strong patient relationships based on real and enduring value.

This is evident to the pharmaceutical industry—nearly half of pharmaceutical manufacturers are now actively using social media to engage with patients on healthcare-related topics, according to a 2014 report released by the IMS Institute for Healthcare Informatics.[3]

The Rise of The Empowered Patient

Sarah Thornton, a user of the UK's National Health Service (NHS), in a *British Medical Journal* opinion piece,[4] criticized the health service for being strong on rhetoric about "patient led care" but weak on implementation. "Despite the strong rhetoric … there has been no consistent strategy for involving patients," she wrote. "The approach to enabling patients and the general public to have more say about how services are planned and developed has been piecemeal, and the bodies set up to facilitate patient involvement have been transient."

A new healthcare consumer is gaining ground who, having lost trust in many elements of the healthcare system, is becoming more and more prone to taking charge of his/her own treatments.

Meanwhile, a new healthcare consumer is gaining ground, the so-called "empowered patient," a patient who, having lost trust in many elements of the healthcare system (that is, the regulators, healthcare professionals (HCPs), and pharma and biomedical companies), is becoming more and more prone to taking charge of his/her own treatments. In addition, as out-of-pocket expenses rise, patients expect to be properly and independently informed about possible treatment solutions or healthcare services.

At the same time, having faster and more direct access to information over the Internet offers consumers the chance to proactively learn more about their own or their loved ones' diseases and/or disorders, treatment alternative solutions, and to even share their experiences and confront medical issues with other patients throughout the globe.

As a consequence, patients play a crucial role in today's healthcare, and that trend appears poised to escalate and drive further changes in the industry.

Nevertheless, most healthcare organizations publicizing "patient-centricity" are, currently, going no further than providing patients with access to information and offering them tools to complain.

To make patient empowerment a reality, organizations working in the healthcare industry need to develop a comprehensive systematic approach to communicating with patients. Such a patient-centered Digital Health Communication Strategy must be developed and executed to meet the needs of patients and caregivers so that they and their loved ones can lead healthy, productive lives.

A new healthcare consumer is gaining ground who, having lost trust in many elements of the healthcare system, is becoming more and more prone to taking charge of his/her own treatments.

In order to have a better understanding of "why" and "how" patient-centeredness is important, it is necessary to understand the psychology of motivation in human activities. After years of exploring motivational issues among students and employees, social psychologists Edward Deci and Richard Ryan (2002)[5] observed that most people are driven by a need to seek self-determination in thought and action in order to influence the outcomes that affect their everyday lives. When the environment reinforces self-determination, individuals are effective and thrive.

Deci and Ryan (2000)[6] recognized three universal needs that seem to influence the growing of self-determined behavior: the need for autonomy, competence, and psychological relatedness.

The *need for autonomy* is the necessity to perceive actions as coming from internal motivations, not necessarily from external sources. The *need for competency* is the will we all have to learn from the environment and acquire and enhance essential life skills. The *need for relatedness* is the social need to acquire a sense of respect and a strong need to create and maintain social relationships with other individuals. This is especially true when it comes to healthcare.

"Supporting these universal needs lies at the heart of creating an environment that will lead to personal empowerment."

"Supporting these universal needs," Deci and Ryan argued, "lies at the heart of creating an environment that will lead to personal empowerment."

Through patient-centered digital communication, organizations can develop long-term relationships with patients and imbue in them a sense of loyalty. Technology and new media are key elements in this process, but must be used in a way that is transparent and that reinforces the organization's core commitment to providing patients with responsive and continuous support.

"Supporting these universal needs lies at the heart of creating an environment that will lead to personal empowerment."

Defining Digital Health Communication

The advent of the Internet and particularly Social Media has added a new dimension to the discipline of marketing and health communication, which has traditionally relied on TV, print, radio, outdoor, and word-of-mouth (WOM). When we talk about "digital" health communication, we are referring to communication delivered via any of the following "channels:"

- basic Internet websites;

- e-mail;

- social media (Facebook, Twitter, Tumblr, Instagram, and so on);

- online video (for example, YouTube);

- mobile, including SMS (text messaging) and apps;

- any other digital channel that may be developed in the future (for example, the Apple Watch).

While the use of social media platforms in healthcare is evolving, mobile apps are becoming more prevalent and, if well developed and managed, provide easy and efficient ways to help patients manage their health goals and research treatment options. Nevertheless, to date, most efforts in apps development have been in the overall wellness category with diet and exercise apps accounting for the majority available. According to the IMS Institute for Healthcare Informatics report: "An assessment finds that healthcare apps available today have both limited and simple functionality—the majority does little more than provide information."[7]

Health and technology are converging to become ubiquitous in patients' and physicians' lives. This intersection of health and technology is changing how long-term chronic conditions can be monitored and treated. Smart watches are forecast to revolutionize treatment for chronic conditions. Several Silicon Valley and other technology companies such as Google and Samsung are currently investing in mobile health hardware and applications. Apple, for example, introduced HealthKit, a new app bundled with iOS 8 that's designed to give users an easy-to-read dashboard of their health and fitness data, including data from Mayo Clinic and other healthcare organizations and institutions.

The Internet of Things (IoT) is becoming more and more personal. Devices like wearables (that is, Nike's FuelBand tracks a person's active life), ingestibles (that is, sensors to be swallowed to help track a person's health), and implantables (that is, cochlear implants or bladder stimulators) are more and more at hand.

In many ways, the rationale of the information revolution has originated from a collective need to achieve autonomy in behavior and thought (Markoff, 2006).[8] At its core, the personal computer revolution has been a change aimed at ripping power away from centralized gatekeepers, and then putting that power back into the hands of individuals for personal action (Toffler, 1990).[9]

Consequently, it is easy to see why individuals are getting involved with the Internet as a means to recover individual autonomy in their own personal health problems.

At the heart of this bootstrapped transformation lies collaboration. In fact, what is new about the evolution of new media technologies in the era of Web 2.0 is the development of highly successful "architectures for participation" (Parker et al., 2009).[10]

Before discussing how to develop and implement a successful digital communication strategy, we need to clarify the definition of health communication and its impact on healthcare outcomes.

As stated by Oaul R. Gully (2009):[11]

> *Communication is at the heart of health care and health promotion. Given that most people are driven by the need to influence factors that affect their lives, it can be assumed that they will, where possible, respond to improved access to health information to make better-informed decisions. For their part, health professionals understand that the information that an individual needs is not limited to that provided in a clinic or hospital. More equal access to information, advice, and support through electronic means can be foundation of partnership that leads to higher-quality care and improved public health.*

Health communication can be defined as "the production and exchange of information to inform, influence or motivate individual, institutional and public audiences about health issues."

Although these definitions, as many others in the literature, may demonstrate the thoughtful nature of health communication, it is also well understood that health communication is indefinable and complicated—in concept and definition, in creation/development and delivery as well as in measurement and management. This is further difficult when looking at health communication in relation to healthcare outcomes (as opposed to consumer goods communication) especially in a business-to-consumer (B2C) context (as opposed to a business-to-business (B2B) environment).

In addition, the distinction between communication and marketing is poorly understood and often unclear. Each method of delivering information offers a different, yet complementary approach to improving health outcomes.

The American Marketing Association defines marketing as "an organizational function and a set of processes for creating, communicating,

Health communication can be defined as "the production and exchange of information to inform, influence or motivate individual, institutional and public audiences about health issues."

and delivering value to customers and for managing customer relationships in ways that benefit the organization and its stakeholders." Marketing communication, or promotion, involves the use of communication to support the marketing process. Specifically, according to Maibach at al. (2007): "Marketing communication is used to inform prospective customers, and business partners, about the availability, benefits, and costs associated with the organization's products and services, and to manage relationships with those key stakeholders. Moreover, the practice of public health communication has been greatly influenced by marketing methods, especially the use of marketing research and adoption of a consumer-orientation." Despite these areas of overlap, Maibach et al. (2007)[12] believe that "marketing and communication are sufficiently distinct—with distinctions that are directly relevant to effective public health practice—as to necessitate that one activity not be considered a sub-set of the other."

One metric by which to determine the relevance of communication and marketing to public health practice is the extent to which they are capable of creating—or contributing to—beneficial changes in each of the five fields of influence synthesized in the People & Places Framework proposed by Maibach et al. (2007) (Figure 1.1) which is based on contemporary ecological models of health that links population health, and population health behavior, to the attributes of the people in the population (as individuals, as social networks, and as communities or populations) and to the attributes of the places, or environments, in which those people live.

Communication and marketing each may have potential to contribute to beneficial changes in all five fields of influence and may have some specific uses, or roles.

When talking about health communication we must also talk about social marketing. Health communication and social marketing may have some differences, but they share a common goal: creating social change by changing people's attitudes, external structures, and/or modifying or eliminating certain behaviors.[13]

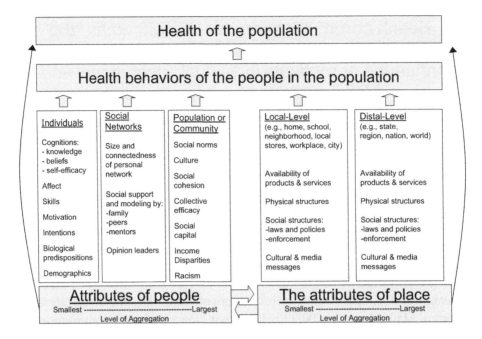

Figure 1.1   A People and Places Framework for public health influence
Source: Maibach et al. (2007).

"Marketing and communication are sufficiently distinct ... as to necessitate that one activity not be considered a sub-set of the other."

According to the Centers for Disease Control and Prevention,[14] "social marketing is the use of marketing principles to influence human behavior in order to improve health or benefit society."

Social marketing planning requires us to understand and incorporate the "Four 'P's of Marketing" (Product, Price, Place, and Promotion) into our program planning. Given the unique nature of health products and services, the implications of these are slightly different. In fact, besides the Product, Price, Place, and Promotion, we now need to look at six new elements unique to the marketing mix in healthcare industry—Patient, Pipeline, Partnerships, People, Physical evidence, and Process. Successful social marketing takes into account all the "Ten P's" and the provision of health services from the viewpoint of the consumer.

Communication and marketing each may have potential to contribute to beneficial changes in all five fields of influence and may have some specific uses, or roles.

Current Challenges to the Healthcare System

Digital communication, while offering opportunities to improve access to healthcare services, patient education, and disease/compliance management, in the medium–long run, is strongly impacting the way healthcare is operating on a global level. All stakeholders will have a number of challenges to face in order to make its potential become a patient-centered reality. Patients, for example, will need to build frameworks that facilitate a healthy dialogue and exchange of information and emotional support to balance their increasing authority. In parallel, the established medical profession will need to recognize the consequences of this evolving dialogue and develop approaches to service delivery that effectively engage with patients on the basis of this rising authority.

At the same time, the biggest challenge for pharma and biomedical companies will be formulating a clear strategy while designing and implementing a new internal and external business model to adapt to the new market environment. In fact, according to the Digital Future 2014 survey,[15] the pharma industry voted "unclear strategy" as the biggest challenge in 2014.

The overall healthcare community, information technology providers, and government institutions will have to face the following main challenges:

- legal and regulatory issues;

- unclear strategy;

- lack of in-house social media monitoring systems;

- lack of internal buy-in;

- ineffective development and use of digital tools;

- low reliability and quality of information available online;

- difficulty of applying traditional quantification of Return on Investment (ROI) to social media campaigns.

To realize the full potential of this digital revolution all stakeholders need to ally and be willing to contribute.

The entire healthcare information infrastructure is currently in a state of change, and we will surely see further changes to the use of computers, the Internet, and ways of collaboration between different stakeholders. Additional channels and usages will emerge in the long run, with platforms like Pinterest, Instagram and Tumblr gaining increasing importance and influence.

These and new future trends will call for healthcare stakeholders collaboration and teamwork in order to find the best ways to use them to their fullest potential and ensure the best outcomes for patients while gaining profits for their organizations.

To realize the full potential of this digital revolution all stakeholders need to ally and be willing to contribute.

The Digital Health Communication Strategy Process

If, in this evolving environment, healthcare organizations will need to focus more and more on delivering holistic services and systems of care, one key to the success of a patient-centered communication program is their effort to improve the patient online experience and engage patients through their website and/or tailor-made digital tools. Specifically, they will need to see health communication as a service or a set of services capable of providing valuable solutions to the new informed and empowered health customer. Pharmaceutical companies, for example, will need to provide "beyond the pill" solutions, and add real value to the patient and to the healthcare outcomes. Smart health communication managers look beyond the attributes of the products and services they offer. By designing and orchestrating several online services, and digital tools, they create a brand experience for patients. The starting point for a successful digital health communication strategy is to realize your existing patient is a healthcare consumer. As a consequence, the Digital Health Communication Strategy Process can be represented in a simple, five-step model (Figure 1.2) adapted from Kotlers' Marketing Process Model. In the first four steps, healthcare organizations act to understand patients, create patient value and build strong patient relationships. In the final step, organizations bring back the rewards of creating superior value. In fact,

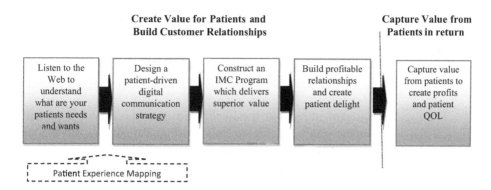

Figure 1.2   A simple model of the Digital Health Communication Strategy Process

Source: Adapted from Kotler, P. and Armstrong, G. (2014), *Principles of Marketing*, 15th edition. Harlow: Pearson Education Limited, p. 27.

by creating value for patients, they consequently capture value from patients in the form of sales (that is, medicines, devices, and health services), profits, improved health and healthcare outcomes, and long-term patient equity.

In this chapter we will explore the steps of this simple model of digital health communication strategy and then develop it more thoroughly in the next chapters. We briefly review each step but focus more on the patient engagement and relationship steps—understanding patients, building patient relationships, and capturing value from patients. We'll look into the second and third steps—designing a patient-driven digital communication strategy and constructing an integrated Health Communication Program that delivers superior value—more thoroughly in Chapters 3, 6, and 7.

... they will need to see health communication as a service or a set of services capable of providing valuable solutions to the new informed and empowered health customer.

UNDERSTANDING THE MARKETPLACE AND CUSTOMER NEEDS

A serious patient communication strategy must start with a comprehensive social media blueprint; that is, listening to the Internet, and not just your company website—the whole Internet. If your company is still depending upon on-site comments as a primary mode of patient communication, then most of the conversation and concerns never make it to you.

The most significant thing that the health industry can do for a patient is to listen to what the patient is saying and writing.

The most significant thing that the health industry can do for a patient is to listen to what the patient is saying and writing. Patients are no longer limiting themselves to complaining on the websites of pharmaceutical/HCPs/institutions—they have decentralized and spread their concerns, ideas, and complaints to anyone who will listen, especially through social media sites such as Facebook, Twitter, and online patient forums.

As you may easily understand, listening to the patient needs and wants is no longer a passive activity. As consumers take advantage of social media to instantly and publicly express their opinions, experiences, and reactions, they expect faster responsiveness from healthcare organizations. Consequently, while you are listening it is critical to promptly and effectively manage the online discussion. We'll read more about this in Chapter 3.

Given the increasing number of patients using the Internet to voice their complaints, that is, chat rooms, complaint-specific websites and disease-related message boards, genuinely concerned companies should at the very least devise technology to "listen" to the chatter that goes on outside of their corporate website.

A successful organization should equip itself with a "social media command center" to monitor Internet activity for customer chatter and questions, while assisting those who need feedback or guidance live, and as it happens.

A properly trained staff taking a similar approach for any organization working in the health industry (that is, pharma, HCPs, and so on) would go a long way to bridging the gap between industry and end user.

Pharma has to be careful about how they plan and implement the listening because there are some laws that mandate their action if they find out about adverse events. Fortunately though, this is not used as an excuse to disengage from patients' comments and concerns that are being registered via social media by some leading pharma companies. The regulation of pharma social media communication is covered in more detail in Chapter 2, "Digital Health Content Regulations, Guidelines and Ethics."

Perhaps the best recent example of effective social media listening from pharma is Sanofi's Diabetes campaign which was launched in 2010 with their Twitter and Facebook profiles, posting news and updates through the respective feeds while direct clinical queries and questions were dealt with via private message. In January 2011, also thanks to the insights from social media listening, the company launched their "Discuss Diabetes" website to collect user tips and inspirational stories. Mobile apps for managing the illness, such as Go Meals,[16] which was developed to help patients get the information and motivation they need to make healthy choices at home or on the go, followed shortly after.

Much like the broader issue of patient adherence, improving communication with the end user and with any stakeholder for that matter cannot be met with a "one-size-fits-all approach." In this age of digital technology, options for dialogue are plentiful; this should be seen as an advantage and not as a chore by the pharma industry.

Like Sanofi for diabetes, truly social brands will listen to what customers are saying and feeling and use that insight to adapt and create products and services.

The Sanofi US Diabetes team was the recipient of the third PharmaGuy Social Media Pioneer Award in 2012 (http://bit.ly/15nJknH). Lack of guidance didn't stop Sanofi from using social media. Nor did a "disgruntled" patient who, in 2010, wreaked havoc on Sanofi via Facebook. When this self-dubbed "Taxoterrorist" attacked Sanofi's Facebook page, did Sanofi hide? Did Sanofi throw up their hands and give up on social media? No. They managed the crisis, they handled it with grace, and they took it one step further: they went public. The team went on record to share his advice and their learnings from the episode.

PATIENT NEEDS, WANTS, AND DEMANDS

We all know that the cost of getting a new patient has become very high. As you must be aware the retention of an existing patient is a far less terrible and costly exercise. What's more, we are faced with the fact that not only is the competitive landscape changing, so is the consumer. Healthcare consumers have changed their wants, needs, and expectations. The organizations working in the healthcare industry that understand this implicitly and then deliver to the expectations, needs, and wants of the consumer will do well.

According to a survey of thousands of patients in Germany, Singapore, and the UK, the adoption of digital healthcare services remains low because

... the core features patients expect from their health system are surprisingly ordinary ...

existing services are either low quality or not meeting patients' needs. The survey, conducted by consulting firm McKinsey, included responses from at least 1,000 patients in the three countries.[17]

It can be argued that success in the use of digital communication depends very much on first understanding patients' digital preferences in both channel and service.

Health systems, payers, and providers often think they need to be innovative when designing their digital-service offerings. But the core features patients expect from their health system are surprisingly ordinary: efficiency, better access to information, integration with other channels, and the availability of a real person if the digital service doesn't give them what they need. Highly innovative services, better apps, and more social media are far less important to most patients (Figure 1.3).

Surprisingly, across the globe, most people want the same thing: assistance with routine tasks and navigating the often-complex healthcare system. In Germany, Singapore, and the UK, for example—three very different countries with three very different health systems—patients most often cite "finding and scheduling physician appointments" as the service with which they need assistance. Other commonly cited needs include help selecting the right specialist and support for repetitive administrative tasks such as prescription refills. What most of these services have in common is that they do not require enormous IT investments to be developed and provided.

The "new normal" for patients includes a stronger and more proactive participation in personal health matters. More than ever, the role of the patient is that of an "informed consumer."

The starting point for a successful digital health communication strategy is to realize *your existing patient is a healthcare consumer.*

This will help you fully realize the implications for your existing patients and allow you to design strategies that will be effective in satisfying their needs and achieving better health outcomes. But satisfying their needs is hardly enough. To improve outcomes, you should be aiming for astonishment with

Ranking of criteria for success of online proposition,[1]
top 3 criteria, %

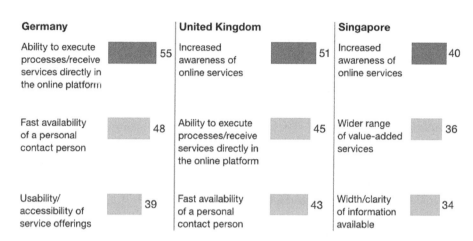

Germany

Ability to execute processes/receive services directly in the online platform — 55

Fast availability of a personal contact person — 48

Usability/ accessibility of service offerings — 39

United Kingdom

Increased awareness of online services — 51

Ability to execute processes/receive services directly in the online platform — 45

Fast availability of a personal contact person — 43

Singapore

Increased awareness of online services — 40

Wider range of value-added services — 36

Width/clarity of information available — 34

[1] Respondents were asked the following: *From your perspective, what needs to happen for you to use certain services online/on your mobile phone more frequently than in the past? Please select the three most important criteria for you.*

Figure 1.3   Ranking of criteria for success of online proposition, top three criteria, %

Source: Exhibit from "Healthcare's digital future," July 2014, McKinsey & Company, www.mckinsey.com/insights. Copyright © 2014 McKinsey & Company. All rights reserved. Reprinted by permission.

The starting point for a successful digital health communication strategy is to realize *your existing patient is a healthcare consumer.*

your level of care and service. Because then those patients will generate better health and quality of life for themselves, and referrals, testimonials, and new customer acquisition will automatically come.

As previously said, experience is what drives online and offline advocacy, so in order for your existing patients to become advocates you need to deliver them that experience not only through your products but also through effective and valued communication tools and contents. In order to design the experience expected by the patient we will need to discuss it with our patients and analyze their answers. One thing that we quickly learn is that their perception of quality of care or innovation is perhaps not aligned with ours.

EXPERIENCES, ORGANIZATIONS, PLACES, INFORMATION, AND IDEAS AS MARKET OFFERINGS

Many organizations make the mistake of paying more attention to the specific products they offer (that is, drugs, devices) than to the benefits and experiences produced by these products and the communication tools/activities developed for them. These organizations suffer from *marketing myopia.* They are so captured by their products that they focus only on existing wants and lose sight of underlying patient needs. They forget that a product is only a tool to solve a patient problem.[18] A manufacturer of a cancer drug may think that the customer needs a drug. But what the patient really needs, besides healing from cancer, is quality of life, convenience, comfort, transparent information, support, and reassurance. These manufacturers will have trouble if a new product is introduced that serves the same customer's needs better or less expensively. The patient will have the same need but will want the new product.

Smart health communication managers look beyond the attributes of the products and services they sell/offer. By designing and orchestrating several online services and digital tools, they create a brand experience for patients. Health-related IoT technologies are just a trivial part of the problem for the Digital Revolution that the healthcare industry is facing while it navigates a chaotic landscape. Specifically for pharma companies, the time of rich pipelines and blockbusters ended long ago. In addition, generics are gaining more and more ground. And with a patient more informed, empowered, and, consequently, more demanding, pharma companies will need to focus more and more on creating value "beyond the pill." This implies having a long-sighted approach and a move, for example, to a range of value-added services, most of which can be digital. "Beyond-the-pill is a logical and inevitable path forward for all," reports Joseph Jimenez, CEO of Swiss healthcare company Novartis in an interview with Bloomberg (2014) for *Forbes Magazine.*[19] "Creating value by embedding products into a holistic offering with the aim to improve patient outcomes and provide tangible competitive advantages."

With an ever-rising "online generation" and continued growth of smart devices, it seems logical that customer service follows suit and gets social.

In a recent *Harvard Business Review* blog,[20] a survey of social media users suggested that speed of response was critical to "social support" success and that the user expectation is to see a response within hours. The article does go on to say that 30 percent of social media users surveyed prefer this technology to using the phone. The financial benefits are clear also, with the study citing a social support interaction costing less than $1, compared to e-mail ($2.50–$5.00) and telephone ($6).

Smart health communication managers look beyond the attributes of the products and services they sell/offer.

As an example,[21] patients familiar with technology at a Sutton Coldfield hospital can give feedback on their treatment and stay via smartphone. The Heart of England NHS Foundation which runs Good Hope Hospital in Sutton Coldfield has released a new Heart of England NHS Foundation Trust (HEFT) Patient Feedback app for Apple iPhones and an Android app available via the Google Play store. The free app is designed to create a communication channel between patients and the hospital to promptly give their thoughts on visiting an area of the hospital or staying on a ward. They can rate the ward on their experience, offer their thoughts and suggestions, and even get in touch with Trust Board members. The message, which is anonymous, will be addressed and responded to within 48 hours as part of the hospital's commitment to openness and transparency. The response will then appear within the app.

PATIENT VALUE AND SATISFACTION

Healthcare satisfaction data focuses, most of the time, exclusively on functional needs—and does not consider emotional needs. In order to create interest, healthcare communicators must focus on both functional and emotional needs.

Focusing holistically and intimately on the patients, their families, and their referring physicians' experiences is central in building the kind of relationship required to engage them and generate value.

Understanding the entire patient journey is important in supporting people who, for example, go through compliance management programs. Having patient insights allows the creation of better apps, as well as a better integration of those apps into EMRs. There is quite a lot of variation in physicians enrolling patients in compliance management programs. One of the key things to change is knowing whether they ask the right questions, whether the app they're using has been incorporated into the workflow, whether it's easy to use, and so on. Once you know if there is a problem and where it is, you can bring in health technology specialists to help the group incorporate the app into the EMR, so it's easier to use and takes less of the physician's time. Simultaneously, you will develop the relationship among patients/carers, physicians, and your brand, required to engage all actors involved in the journey.

You will need to see things through someone else's eyes, and, consequently, to put yourself in that person's shoes. Toward this aim, "experience mapping" can be a very useful tool to help hospitals and pharma/biomedical/life sciences organizations find out what patients really think and feel about their healthcare experience. The concept of "experience mapping" was first introduced by website developers to determine online users' experience as they moved from page to page. It is different from process mapping and traditional patient satisfaction research, which help organizations understand the customer experience at each step in the process from beginning to end. Experience mapping helps develop a strong customer-centric focus. It is a strategic change in focus from operations to customer. It explains the emotions behind the actions. It is most valuable when customer relationships are complex and involve multiple "touch points" or points of contact—perfect for hospitals or health management for drugs/biomedical products/devices.

More specifically, it is an in-depth qualitative research technique utilizing a visual cue (The Experience Map) to help patients, their family members, and their referring physicians recall specific episodes in their journey (Figure 1.4). Many studies show that direct and actual patient (or physician) feedback provides the best insights into understanding, improving, and managing the experience. Experience mapping enables organizations to evaluate the most important touch points, functional needs, and emotional needs at each step of the journey.[22]

To summarize, the main actions involved in experience mapping (Experience Mapping Process) are:

- identify the key steps before, during, and after a patient visits the facility;

- determine the activities patients and families go through at each step;

- assess which type of touch point delivers the brand's promise for each activity;

- talk to patients and families about their functional and emotional needs at each step;

- consolidate the findings into a "Voice of the Customer" report;

- determine the priorities of touch points and performance of each;

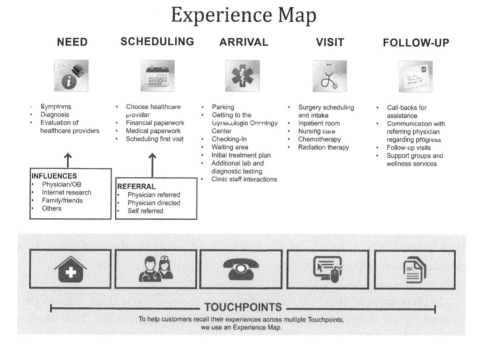

Figure 1.4 **Example of a patient experience map cataloging the stages of the patient journey**

Source: Gelb Consulting Healthcare.

- identify key opportunities for improvement in care, coordination, and communication;

- review patient stories to identify candidates for testimonials;

- develop meaningful messages by understanding attitudes, differentiators, and reasons to believe.

Designing a Patient-Centered Digital Strategy

Once healthcare communication managers and marketers fully understand patients and the healthcare market, they can design a patient-driven marketing strategy. Health communication management can be defined as the art and science of choosing target audiences and building profitable relationships with them. The health communication manager's aim is to find, listen, and engage a clearly defined and understood audience with the objective of improving healthcare outcomes by creating, delivering, and communicating superior customer value. To design a winning marketing strategy, the health communication manager must answer two important questions: What patients will we serve (what's our target market)? And how can we serve these patients best (what's our value proposition)? We'll discuss these digital communication strategy concepts briefly here and then look at them in more detail in Part 3.

CHOOSING A VALUE PROPOSITION

The organization must also decide how it will serve targeted patients—how it will differentiate and position in the marketplace. *A value proposition is a clear statement of the tangible results a customer gets from using your products or services.*

A strong value proposition is specific, often citing numbers or percentages. It may include a quick synopsis of your work with similar customers as a demonstration of your capability.

In pharmaceuticals, for example, the value proposition is always developed around a clear definition of the benefits provided by a medicine. This implies having either a "disease modification approach," when a medicine is able to change the course of the disease or treat the original cause (that is, Alzheimer's or Parkinson's) or a "symptoms/potential risks reduction approach" (that is, pain and emophilia) treatments. These are examples of how it is possible to build a value proposition that is appealing to both payers and patients. Other examples of value propositions include improved packaging (that is, patient-friendly packages or medicine quantity more flexible to adapt to dosage prescribed), improved delivery or dosage of a medicine—for example, having to take an osteoporosis treatment once a month can also significantly help compliance and thereby improve outcomes.[23]

When formulating a patient-centered digital communication strategy organizations must make sure to develop their value proposition around the benefits provided by the mix of online/offline tailormade tools and services. This implies, for example, having either a "disease prevention approach" or a "disease management approach".

Preparing an Integrated Marketing Communication Plan

The organization's digital health communication strategy outlines which customers/patients it will target and how it will create value for these customers/patients.

Once all the patient touch points are clear it is clear that focusing only on digital won't be enough, you will need to design an integrated communication plan that includes both online and offline tactics/tools.

The first step to integration is to analyze your existing set of tools and channels (that is, website, blog, e-mail newsletter(s), paper magazine or newsletter, direct mailing, Facebook, Twitter, YouTube).

Having an effective integrated communication strategy requires that you understand how each type of media relates to the other and that you have a program that ensures they strengthen and complement each other to generate patient value.

In order to avoid the "using everything" mistake, it is important to have a clear understanding of the strengths and distinctive features of each channel before getting too far trying to integrate different communication channels you need.

Planning is crucial to integration. Step back and look at each year as a whole. What are the big events that will shape your communication? Is there an awareness week or other national campaign you usually get involved in?

Last but not least, ensure that you are tracking your progress.

Once all the patient touch points are clear it is clear that focusing only on digital won't be enough, ...

Tracking progress not only justifies all of your work to others but it also helps keep you motivated and focused on strategic goals. You should tailor your key performance indicators (KPIs) to your organization, but it is recommended that you review them on a monthly basis, ideally with a wider team in the organization.

Building Patient Relationships

The first three steps in the digital communication process—understanding where the patients meet and what their needs and wants are, designing a patient-driven marketing strategy, and constructing an integrated communication program—all lead up to the fourth and most important step: building and managing profitable patient relationships.

PROVIDER–PATIENT RELATIONSHIP

The relationship between provider and patient forms the foundation of healthcare and is vitally important to both parties. It is the vehicle for sharing information, feelings, and concerns; a crucial factor in the success of treatment; and an essential component in the satisfaction of both patient and practitioner.

Nevertheless, cost-containment efforts, pressures for higher productivity, a managerial rather than professional perspective on healthcare, and increased dependence on technology all have the potential to prevent the capacity of practitioners to develop and demonstrate effective, caring relationships with their patients.

In recent years, effective communication has been found to produce better health outcomes, a greater probability that patients will follow recommendations, and a reduced risk of malpractice suits. These are particularly significant considering the increasing emphasis in the contemporary healthcare system on improving quality and outcomes, increasing patient satisfaction, and reducing or containing costs.

Some basic strategies useful to create effective online relationships are:[24]

- *Offer information that is relevant and valuable for the patients.* Though this may sound easy, most of the HCP websites today miss this important/critical point. They provide a lot of information, often even too much—but little of what consumers consider to be valued.

- *Pay attention to designing and offering patient care key services.* A valuable Web strategy starts by providing complete information, including online experience tools, about the key services the HCP provides.

- *Be consistent and provide the promised online services.* Different to print media and television, websites can truly and effectively provide services (see the CC case history).

- *Involve nurses, clinicians, and any other caregivers who bring the patients in the website.* A HCP's website will be of little value if it neglects the input, awareness, and ownership of physicians and other clinicians. In fact, the best way to attract qualified users (a local person dealing with a medical or health problem) is to make sure that physicians and other caregivers have been actively involved in the development of the information on the site so that they can advocate it to their patients.

- *Start an online relationship with a "signal event."* A "signal event" happens when a patient is initially being informed about a health condition that is possibly going to change his/her life. Regardless of it being positive (a woman learns that she is pregnant) or negative (a man learns he has cancer) the person involved will be highly motivated to seek information concerning the medical condition and its treatment options.

- Use a "clicks and mortar" approach to your web services. A website's design and content should be designed with the aim of turning health information seekers into service users in case of need.

INDUSTRY–PATIENT RELATIONSHIP

Companies marketing drugs and medical devices very often talk the language of patient-centricity but rarely do they concretely and effectively provide it. Constrained by regulations in many countries limiting what can, and cannot, be communicated to patients or divulged to the public, industry has battled for years to obtain more openness with regulatory regimes that actively limit its possibility to communicate with end user customers.

Whatever industry does, it will have to face the concern that when profit is part of the health equation, then its motives can be questioned. The funding of patient groups and related patient-focused initiatives leaves the industry open to the accusation that, by encouraging actions and patient pressure on health payers and Health–Technology Assessment bodies, it can achieve what it is unable to do through normal regulatory channels: advance reimbursement and product use while driving sales.

With the increasing use of the Internet and social media, though, demand for information and dialogue is developing rapidly. The industry's response—whether by choice or regulatory burden—has not yet been effective and completely fulfilling. If the common aims of patients and industry are to be really reciprocally valuable, the industry has to raise its patient–relations game.

PARTNER RELATIONSHIP MANAGEMENT

When it comes to creating customer value and building strong customer relationships, today's health communicators know that they cannot go it alone. They must work closely with a variety of communication partners. In addition to being good at customer relationship management, health communicators must also be good at partner relationship management—working closely with others inside and outside the organization to jointly bring more value to customers.

In today's more connected world, every functional area in the organization can interact with patients. The new accepted wisdom is that—no matter what your job is in a company—you must understand marketing and be patient-focused. Rather than letting each division go its own way, organizations must link all divisions in the cause of creating value. Health communicators must also partner with institutions, patient, and physician associations.

BUILDING PRODUCTIVE RELATIONSHIPS IN THE HEALTHCARE INDUSTRY

At the basis of effective provider–patient/industry–patient relationships lies productive relationships in the industry as a whole. Indeed, though very important in any organization, productive ongoing relationships are often critical in the healthcare industry and even more when dealing with digital communication. In fact, not only can poor relationships and conflict lead to patient suffering or harm, they can also ignite collaborative care-giving which characterizes these type of organizations.

Although we know that relationships are often demanding, especially in high workload or pressure situations, such as healthcare, the fact is that as individuals and organizations we typically take relationships for granted. As a consequence, sooner or later, many of our working relationships need maintenance. They need us to get the right skills to make them work effectively. They need a willingness to adapt, to listen to others, to accept different perspectives and approaches. A good way to think about this is in terms of more relationship "enabling" behavior and less "challenging" behavior as shown in the Table 1.1.[25]

Using this grid can help to quickly turn the situation around in any healthcare organization, even where the current culture is difficult, or relationships are severely strained at individual or functional level (nurses and

Table 1.1   Relationship analysis grid

Enablers	(need more of) listening, patience, clear communication, honest/open communication, cooperation, teamwork
Challengers	(need less of) personal agendas, ego, over-communication, stress, interpersonal conflict, lack of clarity, ambiguity
Sustainers	(create and maintain) openness, assertiveness, effective conflict handling skills, good feedback processes

doctors having ongoing conflict issues for example). The secret is to begin in one area (probably where the problems are at their worst) and use the new behaviors learned to apply more extensively while trust about what works best starts to increase.

Capturing Value from Patients

The final step of the health communication process outlined in Figure 1.2 involves capturing value in return in the form of positive health behavior, healthcare outcomes, and profits. Government, pharmaceutical companies, and managed care alike have a shared goal of helping people live longer and more productive lives. They differ on how to get there, however, there is a shared consensus that improving health can deliver significant economic benefits to society. Loyal patients represent an important asset for government, pharmaceutical companies, and managed care alike. By creating superior patient value, organizations create highly satisfied patients who stay loyal and not only will continue, for example, to choose a hospital practice for their healthcare needs, but can bring new business to it by promoting its services to family and friends. This, in turn, means greater long-run returns for the organization. In this section, we discuss the outcomes of creating customer value: customer loyalty and retention, share of market and share of customer, and patient equity.

DEVELOPING AND MAINTAINING CUSTOMER LOYALTY AND RETENTION

Research shows that consumers feeling better about a company that delivers custom content are also more likely to buy from that company. This means that building customer loyalty through online communication is important for

Government, pharmaceutical companies, and managed care alike have a shared goal of helping people live longer and more productive lives.

medical practices that want to consolidate their position in the community. There are a number of ways to strengthen your online bond with patients to improve retention and grow your brand. Here is a non-exhaustive list of the very basic ones:

- *Listen.* Find a way to analyze negative comments and complaints online.

- *Show your comprehension and encouragement.* You can send a "thank you" e-mail after a patient visits your office, or congratulate the patient on the results reached in managing his/her disease.

- *Be coherent.* Make sure that you offer a coherent online content and service, such as replying to e-mails on the same day.

- *Exceed patients' expectations.* Anticipate their needs. Is your patient affected by diabetes? Provide tasty and healthy recipes through your website or social media.

- *Provide outstanding online customer service.* A follow-up mail to see how a patient is progressing can be just as valuable as the care you provide in your office.

- *Provide valuable tools* to improve compliance and effectively manage their health (that is, mobile apps).

SHARE OF MARKET AND SHARE OF CUSTOMER

Healthcare organizations need to focus on earning their market share, marking the shift from price-extractive growth to value-based growth. For example, increasingly, hospitals will get bigger by being better, reaping the rewards of superior performance in a competitive marketplace. In the up-and-coming era of value-based growth, where patients are wisely buying care in a competitive market, organizations are urged to treat growth as an output and no longer as an input. Hospitals will grow when providing services that meet purchasers' want. Likewise, pharma and biomedical companies will have to directly or indirectly contribute to value creation for a new, more demanding patient and a healthcare system struggling to reduce costs and improve people health. In this scenario, digital solutions can play a central and cost-effective role when supported by a strong and successful health communication strategy.[26]

BUILDING PATIENT EQUITY

It is important not just to acquire patients, but also and mostly, to keep and grow their number as well. Companies not only want to create profitable patients, but to "own" them for life, earn a greater share of their "purchases," and capture their patient lifetime value. What, then, is patient equity?

Patient equity is the total combined patient lifetime values of all of the organization's current and potential patients. Clearly, the more loyal the firm's profitable patients (that is, patients who proactively recommend a HCP's services to others or choose a HCP practice for all their healthcare needs), the higher the firm's patient equity.

Patient equity may be a better measure of an organization's performance than current sales or market share. Whereas sales and market share reflect the past, patient equity suggests the future.

The final goal of patient relationship management (PRM) is to produce high patient equity.

... digital solutions can play a central and cost-effective role when supported by a strong and successful health communication strategy.

Nevertheless, PRM alone won't grow revenues because, for example, it is ten times more expensive to generate revenue from a new patient and it is six times more expensive to service patients through a call center than it is via the Internet and website; patients who refer another patient generate revenue at no cost.

It's time to change: patient management should focus on value creation, not cost reduction, effectiveness, not efficiency. PRM should have revenue targets.

Healthcare organizations must shift from PRM to patient equity management (PEM). That is, Patient Equity/Experience Management is the new Marketing.

Pharmaceutical and biomedical companies should develop and implement, possibly in partnership with HCPs, digital communication initiatives that include a range of value-added services.

Pharmaceutical and biomedical companies should develop and implement, possibly in partnership with HCPs, digital communication initiatives that include a range of value-added services.

This should further motivate pharmaceutical and biomedical companies to develop and implement, possibly in partnership with HCPs, digital communication initiatives that include a range of value-added services.

Actions speak louder than words

Notes

1   http://my.clevelandclinic.org/patients-visitors/patient-experience/programs-services [Accessed 30 September 2014].

2   Gandolf, S. (2014), How Cleveland Clinic Builds Brand Recognition via Multichannel Marketing. Healthcare Success Strategies [online]. Available at http://healthworkscollective.com/stewart-gandolf/198866/how-cleveland-clinic-builds-brand-recognition-multichannel-marketing [Accessed 30 September 2014].

3   IMS Health (2014), Engaging Patients through Social Media Study [online]. Available at http://www.imshealth.com/portal/site/imshealth/menuitem.762a961826a ad98f53c753c71ad8c22a/?vgnextoid=ff71ad0087c73410VgnVCM10000076192ca2RCRD [Accessed September 2014].

4   Thornton, S. (2014), Beyond Rhetoric: We Need a Strategy for Patient Involvement in the Health Service. British Medical Journal [online]. Available at: http://www.bmj.com/content/348/bmj.g4072.long [Accessed 30 September 2014].

5   Deci, E.D. and Ryan, R.M. (2002), *Handbook of Self-determination Research*. New York: University of Rochester Press.

6   Ryan, R.M. and Deci, E.L. (2000), Self-determination Theory and the Facilitation of Intrinsic Motivation, Social Development, and Well-Being. *American Psychologist*, 55, 68–78.

7   IMS Institute for Healthcare Informatics report—October 2013.

8   Markoff, J. (2006), *What the Dormouse Said: How the Sixties Counterculture Shaped the Personal Computer Industry*. London: Penguin Books; Reprint edition.

9   Toffler, A. (1990), *Powershift: Knowledge, Wealth and Violence at the Edge of the 21st Century*. New York: Bantam Books.

10   Parker, J.C. and Thorson E. (2009), *Health Communication in the New Media Landscape*. New York: Springer Publishing Company, p. 142.

11   Gully, O.R. (2009), *Health Communication in the New Media Landscape*, Foreword. New York: Springer Publishing Company, p. xxvii.

12   Maibach, E.W., Abroms, L.C. and Marosits, M (2007), Communication and Marketing as Tools to Cultivate the Public's Health: A Proposed "People and Places" Framework. *BMC Public Health*, 7:88 doi:10.1186/1471–2458–7-88.

13   CDCynergy Social Marketing Edition [online]. Available at http://www.orau.gov/cdcynergy/soc2web/default.htm [Accessed 30 September 2014].

14   Centers for Disease Control and Prevention (2011), What is Health Communication? [online]. Available at http://www.cdc.gov/HealthCommunication/HealthBasics/WhatIsHC.html [Accessed 13 December 2014].

15   PMGroup Worldwide Ltd. (2014), Pharma's Top Digital Challenge in 2014? Strategy [online]. Available at http://www.pmlive.com/blogs/digital_intelligence/archive/2014/january/pharmas_top_digital_challenge_in_2014_strategy [Accessed 13 December 2014].

16   Gomeals [online]. Available at http://www.gomeals.com/ [Accessed 30 September 2014].

17   Biesdorf, S. and Niedermann, F. (2014), Healthcare's Digital Future, McKinsey & Company[online]. Available at www.mckinsey.com/insights [Accessed 30 September 2014].

18   Kotler, P. and Armstrong, G. (2014), *Principles of Marketing,* 15th edition. Harlow: Pearson Education.

19   Bloomberg, J. (2014), Digital Transformation Moves Pharma "Beyond the Pill." *Forbes Magazine* [online]. Available at http://www.forbes.com/sites/jasonbloomberg/2014/08/15/digital-transformation-moves-pharma-beyond-the-pill/ [Accessed 30 September 2014].

20   Benmark, G. and Singer, D. (2012), Turn Customer Care into "Social Care" to Break Away from the Competition, 7:00 AM, December 19, 2012, HBR Blog Network [online]. Available at http://blogs.hbr.org/cs/2012/12/turn_customer_care_into_social.html [Accessed 30 September 2014].

21   Horner, N. (2013), [online]. Available at http://www.lichfieldmercury.co.uk/Patient-engagement-makes-smart/story-20232218-detail/story.html [Accessed 13 December 2014].

22   Gelb Consulting Group, Inc. (2014), Using Experience Mapping to Build Patient Enchantment. This article originally appeared in Healthcare Strategy Alert! Forum for Healthcare Strategists.

23   Besthof, R. (2014), Marketing Analytics Helps Pfizer Deliver Healthy Value Propositions [online]. Available at http://www.argylejournal.com/chief-marketing-

officer/pfizer-leverages-global-research-and-development-to-drive-value-for-customers/#sthash.1sLeIc1r.dpuf [Accessed 15 December 2014].

24   Thomas, C.L. (2002), Seven Strategies for Building Effective Online Relationships. Health Progress, p. 9,56 [online]. Available at https://www.chausa.org/docs/default-source/health-progress/net-gains---seven-strategies-for-building-effective-online-relationships-pdf.pdf?sfvrsn=0 [Accessed 15 December 2014].

25   Warner, J. (2013), Building Productive Relationships in the Healthcare Industry. Climate and Culture [online]. Available at http://blog.readytomanage.com/building-productive-relationships-in-the-healthcare-industry/ [Accessed 15 December 2014].

26   Larezow, R. (2014), Health System Growth Strategy for the Value-Based Market. The Advisory Board Company [online]. Available at http://www.advisory.com/research/health-care-advisory-board/studies/2014/health-system-growth-strategy-for-the-value-based-market [Accessed 15 December 2014].

Chapter 2

Digital Health Content Regulations, Guidelines, and Ethics

JOHN MACK

"The more things change, the more they stay the same."

Consider this tweet made via the @Boehringer Twitter account:

Mirapexin®/Sifrol® prolonged-release, once daily tablet for the treatment of Parkinson's disease approved for EU/EEA http://bit.ly/GNeOw

Does it violate any laws? Is it ethically sound? Does it help patients?

With patients needing and accessing information throughout their patient journey, the relevance and quality of information on the Internet needs to be assured. It is important, therefore, that the information healthcare marketers publish on the Internet meets the highest legal, ethical, and quality standards. Only then will it truly satisfy the needs of patients and physicians and improve health outcomes. In this chapter we'll discuss guidelines for developing and recognizing reliable digital health information no matter the channel, whether it be Web 1.0, user-generated content (UGC) via social media (Web 2.0), or mobile applications.

In 1997, John Mack posted to his blog the cartoon shown in Figure 2.1 with the caption "On the Internet, nobody knows you're a quack." This symbolizes the problem faced by consumers and patients as well as HCPs seeking medical information and advice on the Internet. But it's not just "quack" physicians who peddle snake oil remedies on the Internet. In today's Web 2.0 world consumers and patients can easily post as well as access an enormous amount of health and medical information on the Net, much of it published by individuals and organizations with dubious or unknown credentials. It is often difficult for consumers and even physicians to determine the source of information on the Internet and judge what is "good" and reliable.

Figure 2.1   Quack cartoon

Who do consumers trust online? Poll after poll shows that consumers trust other consumers. A Neilson Buzzmetrics poll[1] claims that consumers trust consumer opinions posted online more than they trust advertising in newspapers, magazines, TV, or radio.

One of the biggest advertisers online and offline is the pharmaceutical industry, at least in the US. It a well-known fact that a majority of consumers lack trust in the pharmaceutical industry: only 34 percent of the patient groups responding to a 2012 PatientView global survey[2] of 600 international, national, and regional patient groups, stated that multinational pharma companies had an "Excellent" or "Good" reputation during the course of that year, compared with 42 percent in 2011—a 19 percent decline.

These results place multinational pharma companies sixth out of seven healthcare organizations for reputation among patients during 2012. Only for-profit health insurers fare worse, with just 24 percent of the 2012 respondent patient groups saying that this healthcare stakeholder has an "Excellent" or "Good" corporate reputation.

So, how can patients trust and judge the credibility of information on the Internet provided by the healthcare industry and separate the wheat from the chaff?

Believe it or not, the US Food & Drug Administration (FDA) was instrumental in bringing this issue into the public for debate in October, 1996, when it hosted its first-ever public hearing on regulation of the pharmaceutical industry on the Internet. The purpose of this two-day gathering was to help the FDA evaluate how "the statutory provisions, regulations, and policies concerning advertising and labeling should be applied to product-related information on the Internet and whether any additional regulations, policies, or guidances are needed."

... how can patients trust and judge the credibility of information on the Internet provided by the healthcare industry and separate the wheat from the chaff?

In attendance at that seminal FDA meeting were many of the people directly responsible for creating the "Medical Internet" at that time. It included representatives from the pharmaceutical industry, advertising and marketing industry, medical associations and publishers, patient advocacy groups, physicians, website developers, and other government agencies such as the Federal Trade Commission (FTC).

This was an important meeting, not just for the pharmaceutical industry, but for all organizations that had a stake in improving the quality of health information on the Internet. The topics for discussion raised many issues related to:

- quality of content;

- commercial behavior;

- privacy, security and confidentiality;

- disclosure;

- use of the Internet in the practice of healthcare provision.

In June, 1997, several participants in the FDA meeting, including John Mack, founded the Internet Healthcare Coalition, which was comprised of the same mix of organizations as was assembled at the FDA hearing. In addition, the Coalition membership was international in scope.

In 2000, the Coalition published the eHealth Code of Ethics[3] for developing credible, quality health information on the Internet. Although these guidelines are focused on what we now call Web 1.0, they are as applicable today as they were "back in the day." See a summary of the Code below.

THE INTERNATIONAL E-HEALTH CODE OF ETHICS (SUMMARY)

Vision Statement:

The Internet is changing how people receive health information and health care. All who use the Internet for health-related purposes must join together to create an environment of trusted relationships to assure high quality information and services, protect privacy, and enhance the value of the Internet for both consumers and providers of health information, products, and services. The goal of the "e-Health Code of Ethics" is to ensure that all people worldwide can confidently, and without risk, realize the full benefits of the Internet to improve their health.

Introduction:

Health information has the potential both to improve health and to do harm. All people who use the Internet for health-related purposes must be able to trust that the sites they visit adhere to the highest ethical standards and that the information provided is credible.

Because health and health care are critically important to people, the organizations and individuals that provide health information on the Internet have special, strong obligations to be trustworthy, provide high quality content, protect users' privacy, and adhere to standards of best practices for online commerce and online professional services in health care.

Guiding Principles

1. Candor and Trustworthiness

    Organizations and individuals providing health information, products, or services on the Internet have an obligation to candidly disclose:

    *   Those factors that could influence content

    *   The potential risks of providing personal information on the Internet.

2. Quality

    Organizations and individuals offering health information, products, or services on the Internet have an obligation to:

    *   Provide high quality information, products, or services

    *   Provide means for users to evaluate the quality of health information.

3. Informed Consent, Privacy and Confidentiality

    Organizations and individuals providing health information, products, or services on the Internet have an obligation to:

    •   Safeguard users' privacy

    •   Obtain users' informed consent when gathering personal information.

4. Best Commercial Practices

    Organizations and individuals who sponsor, promote, or sell health information, products, or services on the Internet have an obligation to:

    •   Disclose any information a reasonable person would believe might influence his or her decision to purchase or use products or services

    •   Be truthful and not deceptive

    •   Engage in responsible business relationships and affiliations

    •   Guarantee editorial independence

    •   Disclose the site's privacy policy and terms of use.

    Online marketers of health products and services should be forthright in any claims about the efficacy, performance, or benefits of products or services and should clearly distinguish content intended to promote or sell a product, service, or organization from educational or scientific content. The standard practice is to label promotional content as an "Advertisement." We'll have more to say about this later.

5. Best Practices for Provision of Health Care on the Internet by Health Care Professionals

    Health care professionals and organizations who provide health information, products, or services on the Internet have an obligation to:

    •   Adhere to the highest standards of professional practice

    •   Help patients to understand how the Internet affects the relationship between professional and patient while adapting the highest professional standards to the evolving interactions made possible by the Internet.

The Coalition also published a list of short tips to help patients and physicians evaluate the reliability of online health information and advice. These tips are still relevant today.

1.   Choosing an online health information resource is like choosing your doctor. You wouldn't go to just any doctor and you may get

All who use the Internet for health-related purposes must join together to create an environment of trusted relationships to assure high quality information and services, protect privacy, and enhance the value of the Internet for both consumers and providers of health information, products, and services.

opinions from several doctors. Therefore you shouldn't rely on just any one Internet site for all your health needs. A good rule of thumb is to find a Web site that has a person, institution or organization in which you already have confidence. If possible, you should seek information from several sources and not rely on a single source of information.

2.   Trust what you see or read on the Internet only if you can validate the source of the information. Authors and contributors should always be identified, along with their affiliations and financial interests, if any, in the content. Phone numbers, e-mail addresses or other contact information should also be provided.

3.   Question Web sites that credit themselves as the sole source of information on a topic as well as sites that disrespect other sources of knowledge.

4.   Don't be fooled by a comprehensive list of links. Any Web site can link to another and this in no way implies endorsement from either site.

5.   Find out if the site is professionally managed and reviewed by an editorial board of experts to ensure that the material is both credible and reliable. Sources used to create the content should be clearly referenced and acknowledged.

6.   Medical knowledge is continually evolving. Make sure that all clinical content includes the date of publication or modification.

7.   Any and all sponsorship, advertising, underwriting, commercial funding arrangements, or potential conflicts should be clearly stated and separated from the editorial content. A good question

to ask is: Does the author or authors have anything to gain from proposing one particular point of view over another?

8.   Avoid any online physician who proposes to diagnose or treat you without a proper physical examination and consultation regarding your medical history.

9.   Read the Web site's privacy statement and make certain that any personal medical or other information you supply will be kept absolutely confidential.

10.   Most importantly, use your common sense! Shop around, always get more than one opinion, be suspicious of miracle cures, and always read the fine print.

Accreditation

The eHealth Code of Ethics is a self-regulatory system. There is no mechanism in place to accredit that websites honor the Code. The HONcode,[4] however, developed by the Health on the Net Foundation (HON), which is a not-for-profit organization founded in 1995 under the auspices of the Geneva Ministry of Health and based in Geneva, Switzerland, does offer a yearly certification program to ensure that sites claiming to follow the Code actually do so. Certified sites display the HONcode emblem (see Figure 2.2).

The HONcode principles are similar to the eHealth Code of Ethics principles:

Principle 1: Authority
Give qualifications of authors.

Principle 2: Complementarity
Information to support, not replace, the relationship that exists between a patient/site visitor and his/her existing physician.

Principle 3: Confidentiality
Respect the privacy of site users.

Figure 2.2   HONcode

Principle 4: Attribution
Cite the sources and dates of medical information.

Principle 5: Justifiability
Any claims relating to the benefits/performance of a specific treatment, commercial product or service will be supported by appropriate, balanced evidence.

Principle 6: Transparency
Accessibility, provide valid contact details.

Principle 7: Financial disclosure
Provide details of funding.

Principle 8: Advertising
If advertising is a source of funding it will be clearly stated. A brief description of the advertising policy adopted by the Web site owners will be displayed on the site. Advertising and other promotional material will be presented to viewers in a manner and context that facilitates differentiation between it and the original material created by the institution operating the site.

The digital world has changed dramatically since the eHealth Code of Ethics and HONcode were first published in 1996. These days, not many digital health publishers have heard of the eHealth Code and few bother to have their content certified by HON. Furthermore, these Codes have not kept pace with the technology. Today, the digital health arena is being dominated more and more by social media and mobile apps.

According to a PwC's Health Research Institute report published in 2012,[5] 42 percent of US consumers view consumer views of medications or treatments, hospitals and other medical facilities, doctors, and health insurers through social media sites. In light of these data, the healthcare industry must embrace social media to not only provide health information to patients and consumers, but also to engage them in two-way conversations and thereby become more "patient-centric." But there is a need for some new "rules" or "best practices" for healthcare communicators to guide them in carrying on these conversations.

Regulatory agencies in Europe and in the US have provided the drug industry with some guidelines about how to engage consumers, patients, and HCPs via social media without violating the law. There are few official guidelines, however, for the industry to follow when publishing mobile health applications. Let's look first at the guidelines for social media. Later we'll take up the issue of mobile health apps.

In the UK and the rest of Europe, it is not legal for pharmaceutical companies to promote brand name prescription drugs to consumers. They are only allowed to promote to licensed health professionals and to send consumers printed information under certain circumstances. There are laws and industry self-regulatory guidelines in the UK that govern how pharma companies can use social media to communicate with health professionals. Let's look at some recently-published guidelines from the Prescription Medicines Code of Practice Authority (PMCPA), which oversees the self-regulatory code of the Association of the British Pharmaceutical Industry (ABPI). PMCPA guidelines published in February, 2014[6] advised the drug industry on how to use online communications and remain compliant with the ABPI Code of Practice.

... there is a need for some new "rules" or "best practices" for healthcare communicators to guide them in carrying on [social media] conversations.

Regarding Twitter, for example, PMCPA has this to say:[7]

> *"If a company wanted to promote a medicine via Twitter it would have to ensure that if the medicine was prescription only, the audience was restricted to health professionals and that the message, in addition to any link to further information, complied with the Code. In addition companies would also have to ensure that recipients had agreed to receive the information. Given these restrictions and the character limit on Twitter, it is highly unlikely that the use of this medium to promote prescription only medicines would meet the requirements of the Code.*
>
> *Using Twitter to alert health professionals about the publication of a study on a medicine is likely to be considered promotion of that medicine."*

An example of a tweet that violated the Code was sent by an agency working on behalf of Gedeon Richter, which is the largest biotechnology and pharmaceutical company based in Hungary. The tweet, which was sent on November 9, 2012, was "Register for the event 'Sharing surgical experience after the use of ulipristal acetate in fibroid patients'."

The PMCPA concluded that this tweet was promotional because it named a prescription-only medicine (ulipristal acetate) and referred to a potential use (in fibroid patients). A breach of the Code was ruled because a prescription-only medicine had been advertised to the public via the tweet.

This is interesting for several reasons.

First, the tweet was not made directly by Gedeon Richter, but by an agency — an events agency — working on behalf of the Gedeon Richter company, which claimed that the tweets were sent without its knowledge or authority.

That excuse didn't wash with the Authority, who noted: "It was an established principle under the Code that pharmaceutical companies were responsible for work undertaken by third parties on their behalf."

Gedeon Richter also tried to convince the Authority that the tweet had a limited audience and therefore was not a promotion that reached the general public. The pharma company said the events company had only 55 followers as of July 2, 2013 and its tweets were only visible to the events company's followers or those who actively sought out the events company's Twitter feed. Also, the tweet was sent at 1.37 AM and therefore Gedeon Richter considered it was extremely unlikely that it would have been received and read by a wide audience.

The Authority was too social media savvy to buy that argument: "The Panel noted that the nature of Twitter was such that tweets could be broadly and quickly disseminated making them available in the public domain and so in that regard the Panel considered that a prescription-only medicine had been advertised to the public."

The main takeaway from this is the lack of oversight by Gedeon Richter over third parties working on its behalf. The PMCPA Panel "was concerned that Gedeon Richter could not identify a contract or other material which clearly set out the role and responsibilities of the events company in relation to the materials at issue. Whilst the Panel accepted that Gedeon Richter had, to a degree, been let down by the third party, it was very concerned that Gedeon Richter had failed to establish a compliance infrastructure for the relationship."

Another reason this case is interesting is that the brand name — Esmya — wasn't mentioned in the tweet, just the scientific name. In its defense, Gedeon Richter noted that another formulation of ulipristal acetate at a different dosage was an entirely different medicine marketed by another manufacturer for a different indication. Gedeon Richter submitted that given the lack of therapeutic indication or any claim, the tweet did not promote a prescription-only medicine. That defense didn't sway the Authority either.

The PMCPA Code, however, is limited to members of the ABPI. Members are only the British affiliates of international pharmaceutical companies. The code does not apply to companies headquartered in other countries. Consider this tweet made via the @Boehringer account:

> *Mirapexin®/Sifrol® prolonged-release, once daily tablet for the treatment of Parkinson's disease approved for EU/EEA http://bit.ly/ GNeOw*

Although this tweet mentioned a brand name prescription drug and could easily be seen by UK citizens, it is allowable because it originated from the @Boehringer account in Germany (not an ABPI member) and not from @BoehringerUK, which is the Twitter account of APBI member Boehringer Ingelheim Ltd UK. Interestingly, similar tweets have been made by FDA. It seems that these new drug approval announcements are the exception to the regulatory rules and are allowable. They also convey important new information that may be of value to consumers.

This example illustrates the problems with laws and regulations that vary from country to country. What is really required is a set of voluntary ethical standards that go beyond local laws and which can be followed by all healthcare organizations no matter where they are located or where they do business. That is why standards such as the eHealth Code of Ethics are still relevant today. Compliance with voluntary guidelines may not resolve the thorny legal issues that challenge the regulated pharmaceutical industry, but it would help improve the trust in the industry to provide quality digital health information.

Meanwhile, back in the States in June, 2014, the US FDA published long-awaited draft guidelines for how the drug industry can comply with regulations when communicating about their FDA-regulated medical products on electronic/digital platforms that are associated with character space limitations, specifically through social media such as Twitter and through online Paid Search (for example, "sponsored links" on search engines such as Google and Yahoo!).

The FDA said promotional drug tweets (and Paid Search ads) have to include everything—benefits AND major side effects (that is, important safety information or ISI)—in the space allotted. Plus, the message—be it tweets or search ads—also must link to "a more complete discussion of the risks" associated with the product. Further, the link must obey these rules:

- it must be a direct hyperlink to a destination (for example, landing page; could be a pdf document) that is devoted exclusively to the communication of risk information about the product;

- it must denote that the landing page is comprised of risk information (even when shortened); and

- the URL should not be "promotional in tone."

What is really required is a set of voluntary ethical standards that go beyond local laws and which can be followed by all healthcare organizations no matter where they are located or where they do business.

According to several industry pundits, regulatory executives, and "regulatory alerts" published by digital agencies, the FDA pretty much blocked pharma marketers from using Twitter and other online venues with space limitations (for example, search engine ads) for meaningful branded Rx promotions.

The door is still open, however, for providing non-branded information via Twitter. The FDA and other governmental regulatory authorities have no jurisdiction over that. Self-regulatory guidelines and eHealth codes of ethics are meant to fill that void.

Aside from Twitter, UGC such as Wikipedia articles, are important sources of health information and advice on the Internet. Health marketers, however, have long expressed their concern that articles about drugs published by Wikipedia may include misinformation. The FDA addressed this issue in another draft guidance document published in June, 2014, titled "Internet/ Social Media Platforms: Correcting Independent Third-Party Misinformation About Prescription Drugs and Medical Devices."[8]

Before we summarize this guidance, it is interesting to note that in comments submitted to the FDA prior to the release of the guidance, the Pharmaceutical

Research and Manufacturers of America (PhRMA) demanded that any edits drug companies make to Wikipedia articles about their products should NOT be subject to FDA regulations at all.

PhRMA said in comments submitted to FDA:[9]

> *FDA should confirm formally that, while it is not possible for manufacturers to monitor or correct all inaccurate information about their products on the Internet, such corrections by manufacturers in response to inaccurate postings will not be considered promotional labeling. FDA's adoption of such a policy would thereby allow manufacturers to correct inaccurate information about their medicines on the Internet or social media (e.g., Wikipedia, Sidewiki, blogs, or other websites) if they should become aware of such information.*

In its guidance, FDA more or less granted this request:

> *When a firm voluntarily undertakes the correction of misinformation in a truthful and non-misleading manner pursuant to the recommendations in this draft guidance, FDA does not intend to object if these voluntary corrections do not satisfy otherwise applicable regulatory requirements, if any.*

... Wikipedia articles, are important sources of health information and advice on the Internet. Health marketers, however, have long expressed their concern that articles about drugs published by Wikipedia may include misinformation.

FDA specifically refers to Wikipedia in Example 11 of the guidance document:

> *A firm finds a webpage about its product that was written by an independent third party on an Internet-based, interactive, collaboratively edited encyclopedia [i.e., Wikipedia]. The firm may choose to contact the author of the webpage and provide corrective information to the author.*

Pharma companies may be able to contact the author of "misinformation" on Wikipedia by leaving a message on the author's talk page or perhaps suggesting edits on the discussion page of the article in question, but these suggestions are likely to be ignored. There's a better way for to correct Wikipedia articles.

In June, 2012, Dr. Bertalan Meskó (@Berci on Twitter), in an open letter to pharma, urged the pharmaceutical industry to employ Wikipedia editors and thus "funnel [their] vast resources" to help.[10]

Berci wrote:

> Based on the pretty negative past encounters between pharma employees and Wikipedia editors (pharma employees trying to edit entries about their own products in a quite non-neutral way), we advise you to employ a Wikipedia editor if you want to make sure only evidence-based information is included in entries about your own products.

"Appointing someone from within your company as a 'spokesperson' in Wikipedia who would perform all edits on behalf of the company is an excellent way to update those entries," said Berci. In a *Pharma Marketing News* survey,[11] 57 percent of respondents agreed that pharma companies should appoint an official Wikipedia editor.

Boehringer Ingelheim (BI) responded to Berci via Twitter: "We look for patient safety issues & react. Its important to stick to Wikipedia policies too, so all transparent." But when asked by Berci if BI had posted anything online about this, BI responded: "No at this point in time we have not … .yet." Nevertheless, Berci remains optimistic.

These days, more and more patients and consumers are accessing the Web via mobile devices and are downloading thousands of mobile health apps. Mobile health apps represent the current "wild west" of digital ethics. "There are tens of thousands of medical, health and fitness apps on the market and their sheer number makes it difficult for health care professionals and consumers to locate apps that operate reliably, are based on valid information, and safeguard users' information," said Happtique CEO Ben Chodor, in a *Pharma Marketing Talk* interview.

Happtique, a subsidiary of the Greater New York Hospital Association's for-profit arm GNYHA Venture, developed a set of standards that it used to certify medical, health, and fitness apps under Happtique's App Certification Program. The purpose of the program was to help users identify apps that meet high operability, privacy, and security standards and are based on reliable content. Unfortunately, the program was suspended after a health IT expert found several security flaws in apps that were randomly selected for evaluation from Happtique's first round of "certified" apps. Certification, therefore, does not appear to be a viable method for improving mobile health app quality.

At a drug industry conference, Carolyn Gauntlett, Senior Innovation Consultant with IMS Health, gave an interesting presentation titled "How to Make Sure You're Getting the Most Out of Your mHealth App Development." Gauntlett pointed out that stakeholders were ready for mobile health apps and a recent European mHealth green paper published on April 10, 2014 noted the role that mobile apps can play in the shift toward patient-centric care. "Healthcare systems will have to open up to the possibility of receiving data from patients (e.g. collected by mobile apps) and ensuring ubiquitous access to care through online health systems accessible by patients and doctors," said the Commission. "This implies a change in the role of professionals who may have to remotely monitor patients and more often interact with them via e-mails."[12]

Mobile health apps represent the current "wild west" of digital ethics.

All the stakeholders are ready:

- policy makers acknowledge benefits;

- the FDA released draft guidelines;

- payers are beginning to reimburse apps;

- physicians recognize the potential and many are recommending apps to their patients;

- patients believe apps will improve healthcare.

"Given this much positivity from stakeholders, why aren't we there yet?" asked Gauntlett. One problem is the profusion of healthcare apps with undocumented efficacy and lacking basic privacy protection.

A 2013 study published in *JAMA Dermatology*[13] found that three out of four smartphone apps designed to be used by consumers to assess melanoma risk incorrectly classified 30 percent or more of melanomas as "unconcerning." The authors suggest that consumer reliance on these applications, which are not subject to regulatory oversight, and not seeking medical consultation, can delay the diagnosis of melanoma and potentially harm users.

Not only consumers, but physicians also are relying more and more on mHealth apps, some of which are designed to assist in making diagnoses. A few of these apps have been evaluated in the peer-reviewed literature, but not all. Even these apps, many of which have been developed by drug companies, can be inaccurate, use undocumented algorithms, or lack the necessary security to protect patient privacy.

Pfizer UK, for example, had to recall a Rheumatology Calculator app because of "a bug in the app ... gives wrong results." This "recalled" app was the most downloaded app tracked by POCKET.MD at the time and although Pfizer sent out a "dear doctor" letter, it is possible that many physicians still used the faulty app many months afterward.[14] Even if no harm was done to patients as a result, trust in Pfizer as an mHealth app developer suffered a setback.

The fourth Annual mHealth App Developer survey[15] cites lack of data security (34 percent) and standards (30 percent) to be the major barriers faced by the mHealth app market. Nearly 40 percent of commercially available free mHealth apps and 30 percent of paid apps sent user data to third parties and did not disclose this in the privacy policy or within the app, according to a report from Mobiquity, a mobile engagement provider. According to a study from Boston Children's Hospital and the University of Cologne in Germany, published in July, 2014, less than a third of the 600 most commonly used health apps in the iTunes and Google Play store had any privacy policy at all in place.[16]

Sooner or later the US Congress or some other governmental agency, perhaps urged on by patient advocates or some health app adverse event, may investigate the mobile health app industry—including the drug industry—to see if further oversight, not just FDA regulations, is required.

Before that happens and to ensure that mobile health apps developed by the healthcare industry—including pharmaceutical manufacturers—are of the highest quality, the industry should differentiate itself from "wild west" developers by being proactive in developing and abiding by a set of "Guiding Principles for Mobile Health Apps." Trade associations such as PhRMA, which has already published guiding principles for consumer advertising and physician interactions, could take the lead here as well.

Here are a few mobile health "Guiding Principles" that the healthcare industry should consider adopting:

- Full Disclosure: Healthcare mobile apps must include full disclosure regarding the company that has created or sponsored the app. This includes contact information. The app should also include appropriate disclaimers and Terms of Use that the user must agree to before the app will run.

- Assure Accuracy: If a healthcare mobile app relies on algorithms or formulas, it must be validated through rigorous testing and documentation to ensure it works properly (that is, calculations are correct).

- Informed Consent/Good Privacy Practices: Personal health data is very sensitive, and the consequences of inappropriate disclosure can be grave. To protect users, if a pharma mobile app collects personal information, it should include a privacy policy that explains how such data is protected (Security), who owns the data, how users can access the data, where data is stored (on the device or on a remote website; that is, the "cloud") and instructions for opting out of data collection.

Nearly 40 percent of commercially available free mHealth apps and 30 percent of paid apps sent user data to third parties and did not disclose this in the privacy policy ...

- Regulatory Compliance: Branded prescription drug mobile apps MUST comply with all applicable laws and regulations. In the US, for example, such branded mobile apps must include important safety information. This information should be presented in an easily accessible manner (for example, on start-up screen). In addition, branded Rx drug apps must be available ONLY from the appropriate US app site (for example, Apple App Store).

- HIPAA Compliance: Mobile apps intended to be used by HCPs in the US that collect patient health data must be HIPAA compliant. Apps for use by non-US physicians must obey similar local laws relating to patient data.

The vast majority—80%—of respondents to the Pharma Mobile App Best Practices Survey,[17] which was hosted by Pharma Marketing News, agree that it is in the drug industry's best interest to police itself and develop best practices or self-regulatory guidelines for developing trustworthy mHealth apps for consumers and physicians. The majority—nearly 80 percent—of 98 respondents to that survey were professionals who work inside pharmaceutical companies or for agencies employed by the pharma industry.

What do patient advocates think about these issues? Most patient advocates who responded to a Truvio/WEGO Health survey sponsored by *Pharma Marketing News* do not trust the drug industry to come up with ethical mHealth Guiding Principles on their own. Obviously, many feel that health apps in general need improvement, not just those developed by pharma. Several advocates suggested that the FDA, the National Institutes of Health (NIH), and patient advocacy organizations should be involved. In any case, if pharma decides to develop guiding principles for its own mHealth products, the industry should be transparent about the process and invite into the discussion patient advocates, HCPs, and at least some of the other stakeholders mentioned.

Fabio Gratton, CEO of Vocalize, which developed Truvio, and the creator of Pocket.MD, which currently tracks over 6,000 industry-sponsored apps said:

> *There is no question that we need some form of guiding principles for industry-sponsored mobile apps, but the unfortunate reality is that no amount of guides or principles can solve the issue of a poorly-conceived app. What I am seeing is companies creating apps that already exist in some similar form—and the rest are mostly brochureware mobile flip-books that never warranted a stand-alone app. While it's understandable that companies can make mistakes, what's not acceptable is not addressing critical issues after they have been reported with crystal clarity on the app store. It's really a shame that a company representative has not been assigned the task of reviewing comments and posting responses. It's really not that hard. In fact, Pocket.MD offers a free tool that allows companies to receive alerts when comments are posted on their apps. This is one area where pharma could really rack up the karma points. Listen, respond, and optimize![18]*

Although Happtique's mobile health app certification program was a failure, it is worth having a look at a few of the standards developed by Happtique.[19]

Content Standard C1 states: "The app is based on one or more credible information sources such as an accepted protocol, published guidelines, evidence-based practice, peer-reviewed journal, etc."

Performance Requirements for Standard C1

- C1.01 If the app is based on content from a recognized source (e.g., guidelines from a public or private entity), documentation (e.g., link to journal article, medical textbook citation) about the information source is provided.

- C1.02 If the app is based on content other than from a recognized source, documentation about how the content was formulated is provided, including information regarding its relevancy and reliability.

Listen, respond, and optimize!

It's pretty easy to find mobile health apps that fail to meet this standard. Janssen Pharmaceutical's "Psoriasis" app for the iPhone and iPad, for example, includes an undocumented "PASI calculator." PASI stands for "Psoriasis Area and Severity Index," which is a tool for the measurement of severity of psoriasis.

But more troubling than the lack of documentation regarding content is the accuracy of the apps software. Happtique Certification Security Standards address this.

Security Standard S6 states: "The app owner has a mechanism to notify end users about apps that are banned or recalled by the app owner or any regulatory entity (e.g., FDA, FTC, FCC)."

Performance Requirements for Standard S6

- S6.01 In the event that an app is banned or recalled, a mechanism or process is in place to notify all users about the ban or recall and render the app inoperable.

- S6.02 In the event that the app constitutes a medical device (e.g., 510(k)) or is regulated by the FDA in any other capacity, the app owner has a policy and a mechanism in place to comply with any and all applicable rules and regulations for purposes of handling all aspects of a product notification or recall, including all corrections and removals.

All certification programs are doomed to fail and/or have limited impact.

I already mentioned the recall of Pfizer UK's Rheumatology Calculator app because of "a bug in the app … gives wrong results."

All certification programs are doomed to fail and/or have limited impact. How can any organization certify the thousands of mHealth apps out there? The task is just too overwhelming. In any case, only a small number of healthcare organizations will be able and willing to pay for certification. The only recourse is self-regulatory standards imposed by industry associations upon its members. Until that happens, each healthcare organization must take it upon itself to assure the quality and accuracy of the mobile health apps it develops. Hopefully, this chapter has provided you with a few tips for how to do that.

Be honest and ethical

Notes

1 Neilson, Global Advertising Consumers Trust Real Friends and Virtual Strangers The Most [online]. Available at http://www.nielsen.com/us/en/insights/news/2009/global-advertising-consumers-trust-real-friends-and-virtual-strangers-the-most.html [Accessed 9 January 2015].

2 PatientView, The Corporate Reputation of Pharma in 2012 [online]. Available at http://www.digitaljournal.com/pr/1613737 [Accessed 9 January 2015].

3 Internet Healthcare Coalition, eHealth Code of Ethics [online]. Available at http://www.ncbi.nlm.nih.gov/pmc/articles/PMC1761853/ [Accessed 9 January 2015].

4 Health on the Net Foundation, HONcode [online]. Available at http://www.hon.ch/HONcode/Webmasters/Conduct.html [Accessed 9 January 2015].

5 PwC Health Research Institute, Social Media "Likes" Healthcare Chart Pack [online]. Available at http://pwchealth.com/cgi-local/hregister.cgi/reg/health-care-social-media-chart-pack.pdf [Accessed 9 January 2015].

6 PMCPA, Digital Communications Guidance [online]. Available at http://www.pmcpa.org.uk/advice/digital%20communications/Documents/PMCPA%20-%20Digital%20Communications%20FEB14%20web.pdf [Accessed 9 January 2015].

7 Pharmaguy, Brits Beat FDA and PhRMA: Issue Social Media Guidance for Pharma, Pharma Marketing Blog [online]. Available at http://pharmamkting.blogspot.com/2011/04/brits-beat-fda-phrma-issue-social-media.html [Accessed 9 January 2015].

8   US Food and Drug Administration, Internet/Social Media Platforms: Correcting Independent Third-Party Misinformation About Prescription Drugs and Medical Devices,[online]. Available at http://www.fda.gov/downloads/drugs/ guidancecomplianceregulatoryinformation/guidances/ucm401079.pdf [Accessed 9 January 2015].

9   Mack, J., The Pros and Cons of Pharma Editing Wikipedia Articles, *Pharma Marketing News* [online]. Available at http://www.news.pharma-mkting.com/pmn116-article02.htm [Accessed 9 January 2015].

10   Webinica, An Open Letter to Pharma: Please Employ a Wikipedian [online]. Available at http://stwem.com/2012/06/13/an-open-letter-to-pharma-please-employ-a-wikipedian-2/ [Accessed 9 January 2015].

11   Mack, J., How Should Pharma Edit Wikipedia Drug Articles?, *Pharma Marketing News* [online]. Available at http://www.surveys.pharma-mkting.com/ WikiSpokesperson.htm [Accessed 9 January 2015].

12   Mack, J., The Sorry State of Pharma mHealth Apps, *Pharma Marketing News* [online]. Available at http://www.pharma-mkting.com/news/pmnews1304-article02.pdf [Accessed 9 January 2015].

13   Wolf, J.A. et al. (2013), Diagnostic Inaccuracy of Smart-phone Applications for Melanoma Detection. *JAMA Dermatology*, 149(4):422–426.

14   Pharmaguy, The First Ever "Dear Doctor" Letter Regarding a Mobile Medical App Recall, Pharma Marketing Blog [online]. Available at http://pharmamkting.blogspot.com/2013/02/the-first-ever-dear-doctor-letter.html [Accessed 9 January 2015].

15   Research2guidance, mHealth App Developer Economics 2014 [online]. Available at http://mhealtheconomics.com/mhealth-developer-economics-report/ [Accessed 9 January 2015].

16   Comstock, J., Study: Less Than a Third of Popular Health Apps Have Privacy Policies, mobihealthnews [online]. Available at http://mobihealthnews.com/36349/ study-less-than-a-third-of-popular-health-apps-have-privacy-policies/ [Accessed 9 January 2015].

17   Pharma Mobile Health App Best Practices Survey, *Pharma Marketing News* [online]. Available at http://www.surveys.pharma-mkting.com/PharmaMobileApps.htm [Accessed 9 January 2015].

18   Mack, J., Patient Activists Demand Higher Quality Mobile Health Apps, *Pharma Marketing News* [online]. Available at http://www.pharma-mkting.com/news/ pmnews1307-article01.pdf [Accessed 9 January 2015].

19   Pharmaguy, Certifying Prescription Grade Smartphone Medical Apps, Pharma Marketing Blog [online]. Available at http://pharmamkting.blogspot.com/2012/08/ certifying-prescription-grade.html [Accessed 9 January 2015].

PART II
Understanding the Marketplace
and Consumers

Chapter 3

Listening to Patients Can Fuel More Personalized Communication

LETIZIA AFFINITO

In the first step of the Digital Health Communication Strategy Process Model, healthcare organizations work to understand patient needs and wants. The Internet offers you the opportunity to do this and also engage with your patient community. Listening and engaging must be an iterative process which never stops. This is how you build great customer experiences.

In this chapter we will explore the definitions of passive and active listening and see how passive listening can be far more action-oriented and intent-filled than it sounds. Both types of listening can lead to a lot of action; after all, isn't that the point of listening? We'll present the type of analysis you need to leverage and possible applications for both passive and active listening. Finally, we will explore how managers gain insights into patients' needs and how companies develop and manage information about important health system elements: patients, competitors, products, and communication programs. To succeed in today's health system companies and organizations must know how to turn mountains of information into fresh customer insights that will help them deliver greater value to customers.

We'll start with a leading case history about listening and engaging in action at UCB, a global biopharmaceutical company focused on delivering superior and sustainable solutions to people who live with severe diseases of the immune and central nervous systems.

Severe diseases, such as epilepsy, Crohn's, or Parkinson's, tend to be "silent diseases"—sufferers are often socially stigmatized and reluctant to share their experiences and insights. To overcome this problem, UCB is creating novel and personal ways for patients and their families to connect, virtually and live, with each other, the organization, its partners, and opinion formers.

UCB's Approach Focuses on Creating "Real Value" for the Patient

UCB is the first biopharma company to sponsor and participate in an open online patient community and proactively handle any adverse events reported on the site.

In 2010, UCB partnered with PatientsLikeMe to create an online, open epilepsy community that captured real world experiences of people living with epilepsy in the US. Part of this partnership included a pharmacovigilance program to monitor the site for adverse events and report directly to the FDA adverse events associated with UCB products. The PatientsLikeMe "platform" is, in fact, designed to collect, analyze, and reflect information received from people with various diseases—including epilepsy—regardless of their diagnosis, prognosis, or treatment regimen. It's great platform for patients to engage with each other, help and support each other and, sometimes, discuss drug side effects and adverse events.

"Social media provides us with a unique opportunity to engage directly with patients. Patients are actively seeking information online and reaching out to social networks. It's definitely more challenging for a highly regulated industry such as ours; however the opportunity to learn from patients and better serve their needs is critical. We know the rules, so we must ensure we work within them," said Trish Nettleship, Director, Social Media & Influence, UCB, Inc., during an interview with John Mack in November 2013.

The industry is concerned about the potential consequences of getting involved in social media.

> "We saw that in 2011, when Facebook changed the rules and required pages to open up commenting; there were many that chose to close pages," said Nettleship. "After careful consideration and planning, we chose to move forward with an open community and embrace the dialogue

with patients. We were in the same boat as everybody else—definitely focused on ensuring that we stay within the regulations."

Since UCB is a leader in the epilepsy space, the company saw PatientsLikeMe as an opportunity to engage patients with a partner to help it engage with epilepsy patients and gain a better perspective on their needs. "We got some really great understandings of our patients, what they care about, what their concerns were, and how we might better meet their needs," said Nettleship. "So the listening part was very, very beneficial to us as a company."

Nettleship continued:

"One of the major considerations with moving into social media is the ability to appropriately capture adverse events and the potential for a significant number. Our approach was to prepare for the worst, while hoping for the best. The good news is we did not see the worst. Around 5% of all product mentions were adverse events. A lot of those did not meet the reporting requirements but nevertheless we worked with our pharmacovigilance organization to ensure we didn't miss anything."

Since 2010, UCB as a company has embraced social media as a new way to reach its audiences, from healthcare providers to patients. Social media is becoming a part of how it does business, whether it be from a customer care perspective, messaging to its patients, disease awareness, and so on.

Nettleship said:

"Social media will be part of every aspect of the business at some point. We will become a social organization. My job is to build best practices across the organization. The online listening space was one of the first things I wanted to focus on because I saw that as the biggest opportunity in the beginning. We started with a global approach to passive listening to get an understanding of what our patients care about, what's important to them, what are their unmet needs, and how we can potentially help them."

"When you talk about brand mentions for our company, as many as 5% to 7% of all mentions can be potentially adverse event related. Having a strong partnership with our pharmacovigilance team

helps prepare for that," said Nettleship. "But we embrace these conversations, because we want to know what is happening with our patients."

Regarding the benefits she adds:

"It's enormous what we're able to understand about our patients and what's happening in real time. We're seeing trends as they are happening, which we did not have access to before. Our agencies did a good job in giving us information, but it was every quarter or every six months. Now that we are actively participating, we see what's happening in real time."

Critical to the success of UCB approach has been:

- *To create and manage private engaged patient communities on social media sites and online patient forums that they sponsor, facilitate, or run.* We just discussed the UCB-sponsored epilepsy patient community on PatientsLikeMe. Another example is UCB's More Than Motion Facebook page, which is devoted to Parkinson's disease. The idea is to drive the conversation outside of just the motor symptoms because there is much more to Parkinson's than just the motor symptoms. Many Parkinson's disease patients are homebound and use online communities to achieve much-needed connections with the outside world. Having that feeling of being connected with what is happening outside their four walls is pretty significant for them. UCB was able to bring real world events to them within their community and it drove significant conversation and engagement with that community.

- *To appoint, for each patient community, a community manager who participates in the online listening and has a sense of what's important in the community.* The community manager posts content that means something to the members. It's a win–win for UCB and the patients. They are delivering content and conversation that's important to them based on what their needs are. As a result, the company has a better understanding what the patient needs and can deliver better products and services to meet those needs.

"Obviously at the end of the day if I can't take what's important to the patient and match that back to a business objective then I am not going to be successful. We can do all the disease state things we want and that is a priority for us, but we have to be able to match that to the business objective," said Nettleship.

- *To integrate online and offline market research. UCB uses online tools to get instant feedback via one-on-one or focus group interactions.* Quick online polls of patients are very cost-effective compared to physical world focus groups. It is often not necessary to do full-blown primary research to understand some issues that can be learned via social media by just listening or asking directly.

- *To properly balance use of technology and human interaction.* For example, drug companies use technology platforms such as Radian6 to monitor online conversations across many social media channels based on a combination of key words including brand names. So it's possible to see how often a brand name drug is mention and in what context—is it a positive or negative comment, for example. Technology can help discover potential dangerous side effects, but human beings must intervene to look at the filtered information and determine if there is an engagement opportunity, or whether it is an adverse event that needs to be reported, or just a product complaint, or something else that the company can help with.

  "We can't assume technology is going to be able to filter it all and just feed it into an automated system," said Nettleship. "If you do that, you will see some pretty significant fails and I've seen it before with automated engagement online. There are some other companies with brands out there who automate their engagement. That's not the best experience for people. So we have to be careful to avoid that."

- *To respond real time (same day) to direct inquiries from the people in their communities.*

  "The expectation today is same day response. Anything longer than that doesn't meet the expectations of today's consumers," said Nettleship.

"So we had to change that model quickly but within a highly regulated environment changing the model takes time. It took about six months working with our legal, medical and regulatory teams to figure out how we could start to respond in real time, by which I mean the same day. The minute one of our community managers sees an inquiry, they either already have a response that he can send or from experience knows what he needs to say or gets an approved response the same day. In some cases, we still have to go through medical or legal, but we get expedited reviews. It's been nice to see that evolution from responding in weeks to responding the same day and sometimes within minutes. A benefit of that is our organic reach in our communities has grown significantly as folks are talking more often with us. Having more conversations with our community and driving up engagement is a benefit for the community as well as it is for us."

- *To listen both for brand mentions and any other relevant types of discussions and seeing how that may help patients.* Nettleship adds:

"I will tell you the biggest learnings we get are not in the branded conversations. It's great to know how people feel about our brands but where I learn the most is on the disease side. Many of the conversations in our patient communities don't mention brands. Less than 35% of all conversations in the epilepsy space, for example, actually mention any brand at all. So if we only looked at the branded conversations we would be missing the bulk of the conversation in epilepsy. So we look at the whole disease and what's important to patients beyond the brand."

UCB's policy is not to force their way in and promote their brand.

They just listen and take note of what they're learning. "Quality of life discussions are becoming more and more of the conversations in the severe disease space," said Nettleship. "For Crohn's we serve up recipes and we talk about food quite a bit with that community because that's something that's very important to patients and has an impact on their disease."

- *To successfully gain commitment from brand managers.* Nettleship admits:

"The majority of the work isn't tied directly to a brand or to sales. We look at it as a way to provide value for patients and believe there will be a positive impact on patient outcomes. We have to prove the value that social delivers back into the organization and to the patient."

- *To bring community management inside to have direct care of the relationships with their customers.*

  "I think, for us, outside partners are always going to be important," said Nettleship.

  "We can never be the experts on everything and we need to understand what's important for us to own. Relationships with our customers are important for us to own. So one of the first things I did was bring community management inside. I don't have data analysts on my team so we have folks from partners that help us do that. But we have someone who's in the dashboard every other day looking at trends and conversations. That person can come to us at any point in time and tell us what's happening, what everybody is talking about. I think the key is understanding what's important for the company to own, the core competencies you want to build. We have to figure out what's important for us to own and what's the okay for us to outsource. It's a balancing act."

Obviously, from a regulatory perspective, unbranded communications are much easier for drug and other healthcare companies to deliver. Drug companies, in particular, can do a lot more in the unbranded space than they can do in the branded space, so they typically go there first. But how can drug companies do more to solve people's problems in a branded environment? Nettleship cited a good example.

  "One way to have a direct impact on patients is solve their problems. If a patient is struggling with usage of a product, we can provide a video that shows how to use the product appropriately," said Nettleship. *"We can deliver that on YouTube and direct patients to that video when they express a need. The regulatory environment does make things more challenging, but we work with our legal, regulatory and compliance colleagues to find appropriate paths forward,"* she added. *"We have to find a way to help without crossing the regulatory line, and there's plenty of ways to do that."*

Today, consumers assume that brands are going to help them with problems they're having, regardless of whether the brand is regulated or non-regulated. However, a conversation about a drug brand initiated by the company in an online disease forum is unacceptable even if that's what the community wants. But drug companies can build awareness around a disease without talking about brands.

Successful companies providing products and services in the healthcare industry share a commitment to understanding and satisfying customer needs in well-defined target markets. They understand that to build great patient experiences they need to listen and engage them interactively. Most importantly, they are open to reviewing and adapting their traditional business models and internal processes to focus and involve everyone in the organization to help understand patients, create patient value, and build strong patient relationships (first four steps of the Digital Health Communication Strategy Process).

Passive and Active Listening

There are essentially two types of listening to social media: active and passive. The distinction is very important because it potentially involves using different strategies and tools. Let's start by clarifying what listening means in this context. It could be defined as observing content generated by all users of social media (that is, Facebook, Google Plus Hangouts, TweetChats, LinkedIn Groups) including private citizens, the private sector, nongovernmental organizations, and all levels of governmental–local, state, and federal. Active listening includes all of the above with the added element of interaction.

While marketers have exercised active and passive forms of listening in the past, social media has made both versions more valuable. In fact, social media provides several unique benefits to the practice of listening—especially as it relates to customers.

During passive listening—sometimes called monitoring—a business attempts to understand what is being discussed in the marketplace as though the business were a fly on the wall. It acts as a spectator and remains uninvolved, until and only if direct attention is needed.

Social media has drastically augmented the value of passive listening in two respects. First, passive access to conversations in social media is immediate, digital, and worldwide. Quiet proximity to the discussions is ubiquitous, and the digital chatter becomes manageable, filterable insightful content, assuming the proper tools are in place to hear a mention of your brand/initiative/ organization/service on all relevant social platforms, blogs, ratings and review sites where these conversations land. Second, passive listeners monitoring social media can engage a customer in need, to address dissatisfactions or to tactfully offer tips to those seeking advice.

Consider the UCB example and this scenario. A patient is having problems with how to get a new medicated patch to stick. They are getting frustrated about it because it is impacting the treatment efficacy. One day, frustrated enough, the patient tweets with dismay: "Yuck. The new patch from UCB is worthless … .it doesn't stick and the treatment doesn't work. I'll ask the doctor for a new brand!"

The patient's 108-character opinion is retweeted across thier network. A close friend posts the rant to Facebook. Left unheard and unaddressed, the digital reach of this "did-you-hear" beacon can accelerate across the 40 to 50 top ratings and review sites and blogs.

Unless someone from UCB or a trained doctor/nurse was there to ask if everything was OK, the traditional form of passive listening fails here.

At UCB they have a solution that tells patients exactly how to fix that problem. Listening gives UCB the opportunity to learn about the problem and proactively deliver that solution on YouTube and point folks to that.

It is now possible—indeed advisable—for companies providing products and services in the healthcare industry to pay attention to what and how it is being discussed online.

The trick here is twofold: have the tools in place to listen to all possible social platforms, and most important, understand how and when to tactfully engage and appease that once loyal customer.

It is now possible—indeed advisable—for companies providing products and services in the healthcare industry to pay attention to what and how it is being discussed online.

In contrast to passive listening, active listening is an engaged approach wherein a business proactively creates an opportunity for a customer to give them feedback—usually with the intention of using that feedback to drive an action. With active listening, you pull responses back to you in order to capture value from customers or patients (see Figure 1.2 in Chapter 1).

Perhaps one of the most outstanding examples of active web listening is represented by the Domino's striking "Pizza Turnaround" campaign.[1]

After five years of sluggish or decreasing revenues, Domino's Pizza made a remarkable revolution in its industry, and one that all B2B or B2C organizations, even from the healthcare industry, can learn from.

First, it invited customers to give their sincere opinion. Second, it truly listened to the burning truth about their product (that is, "cardboard crust" and "totally devoid of flavor"). Finally the company reinvented its product "from the crust up." The *turnaround* began with marketing research to become aware of what customers felt and wanted. To acquire further insights into what customers really felt about its pizzas, Domino's decided to start online marketing research. It listened to consumers' online chats and prompted thousands of direct consumer feedback messages via Facebook, Twitter, and other social media. Using the insights gained online, it started a series of old-fashioned, well-established focus groups to involve customers in face-to-face conversations. Rather than covering up the burning results or flaunting them off, Domino's management recognized the problems and tried to solve them. Domino's began by totally reinventing its pizzas. To communicate the changes and to change customer opinions, Domino's launched a $75 million "Pizza Turnaround" promotion campaign: the research itself was the message. The surprisingly straightforward campaign was entirely integrated into the brand's Facebook and Twitter pages, where the company posted both the bad and the good and asked for continuing opinion and advice. The entire *turnaround* story—from biting focus group footage to the shocked reactions of Domino's executives and hard work to reinvent the product—was edited in a forthright four-and-half minute behind-the-scenes documentary which was published on the website www.pizzaturnaround.com visible for all to see. The campaign was risky but, considering the results, the straightforward approach worked. The transparent ads and message seized consumer interest and changed opinions. The message for marketers from any industry is that having a constructive conversation with customers, listening to their opinions, and, most of all, effectively using the resulting insights can generate significant outcomes.

If the fundamental goal of any organization providing products and services in the healthcare industry is to fulfill the needs of its patients then it is critically important to listen to them and understand their needs. When you get to know patients' needs, you have higher and better chances to include valuable tools and tactics in your digital communication campaign and so provide value for your customer or patient while, at the same time, boosting profits for your organization.

When you get to know patients' needs, you have higher and better chances to include valuable tools and tactics in your digital communication campaign...

Social media has created more valuable forms of both passive and active listening, resulting in a better understanding of the patient. Find out what your patients need, give it to them, and bring in the rewards. It starts with listening.

Developing an internal social media listening capability, besides providing you with useful insights to do something about, can also improve the reputation of the social media department within the company as a whole. Particularly with regard to pharmaceutical companies, centralized listening capability could reduce the threat of communication silos and create synergies across the business.

Online Communities: Public, Gated or a Hybrid?

Online communities, now a very popular means of interaction for people who know each other offline or have met online, can take a number of forms such as chat rooms, forums, video games, blogs and virtual worlds, e-mail lists, or discussion boards. Online communities can "meet" around a common interest and can unfold across multiple websites.[2]

Once they have decided to go for an online community, organizations must decide which kind of community best meets its objectives: public, gated, or a hybrid (largely public with a private, members-only area). Choosing one type of community over another will impact any single aspect of how it will work and, most of the times, even its success.

This fundamental decision depends basically on the characteristics of the audience the organization is planning to serve. For example, a public community is the right format to reach broad audiences. A private, gated community would probably work better to reach a small and focused audience. A hybrid format would better work in the case of multiple audience types or needs. Each type can have different benefits, risks, and type of members (Table 3.1).[3]

Table 3.1   Main features to consider when choosing an online community

	Organization's Need	Members	Benefits	Risks
Public Online Communities	Engage a large audience of consumers or customers	Open to anyone on the web willing to join the conversation on a specific topic of interest	Wide reach, allows organizations to meet market penetration, product or service advocacy	Loss of brand or message control
Private Online Communities (POC) (Gated or invitation-only)	Create a sense of trust and intimacy among members Greater amount of insights about single members Shared acceptance criteria	Involves a highly targeted audience	Higher customer loyalty Higher client penetration of product and service purchases Better R&D and shorter time to market Get high-level expertise from members Market foresight	Members expect higher levels of service Members selection criteria may limit final size High-quality content required Active community management required
Hybrid Online Communities (Both public and gated or private area within the whole community structure. Access determined by the members role. For example, an open, public area for patients with private, gated areas for HCPs and other medical professionals)	Need to serve a need or segment different from the one around which a public or private community has been developed and managed	Involves both a public (anyone) and a private (selective and targeted) membership	Rewards of both having a private member-driven community and using very selective delivery of private content to attract a larger audience to the public space	

Setting Up and Managing a Private Online Community

Private online communities (POCs) are dedicated, brand-sponsored platforms that allow the exchange of ideas and content via a suite of interactive features, like discussion forums, polls, libraries, and member directories.

POCs can be categorized in four types:

- *Innovation centers*: set up to obtain in-depth interaction with customers and partners, these communities aim to share information, gather insights, and act upon community-sourced ideas.

- *Customer huggers*: set up to support members needing assistance, they are short on deep interactions and collaboration with members. Consequently, valued insights stay unexplored.

- *Marketing speakers*: designed and managed most often to maximize Search Engine Optimization (SEO). These communities generate little interaction but aim to communicate a brand's attributes to potential and existing customers.

- *Lead generators*: set up by brands with the aim to involve members in conversations exclusively to generate sales leads. Whenever a potential customer joins the conversation the sales team jumps in to push the sale, stimulating neither confidence nor commitment.

Overall, successful online communities often bring together aspects of each of these four types, nevertheless, healthcare organizations must prioritize the first two styles (customer huggers and innovation centers) which offer brands the greatest potential to source content.

Online communities for engagement and community panels can be differentiated by the number of members they contain—ideally between 200–500 for co-creation and more than 1,000 members for community panels (Digital MR, 2012).[4] Large communities can also be used for quantitative online research in addition to using sub-communities for co-creation.

Owning the sample in a POC or community panel means that you only pay for sample acquisition and can then use it as and when required.

Panels and communities are quite distinct. Put simply, a panel is a group of consumers that a client will conduct surveys with—perhaps once a month or so. The client asks questions and panelists give their answers in a fairly structured way.

However, with a POC, not only can clients ask their community members questions using qualitative and quantitative research techniques, but also members can interact with the client (or host) and among themselves. The nature of the community allows them to do this in a much more unstructured and ad hoc way. Opening up these boundaries and restrictions posed by more conventional research enables communities to get you closer to your customers.

According to a social media study from Elsevier (2012),[5] online patient communities are not particularly popular among physicians. In fact, almost one-third of those interviewed thought they would be unlikely to ever use this form of social media.

One of the primary findings from the Elsevier study is that physicians seem to be more optimistic on using social media tools to interact with each other and that more than three-quarters of all physicians are likely to be involved in online physician communities over the coming five years. HCPs are currently using online physician communities (that is, SERMO) as a virtual form of "doctor's lounge," where they can discuss challenging patient issues with physicians who may have experienced similar concerns. These forms of social media offer instant contact for physicians to consult and exchange on current medical topics.

Opening up these boundaries and restrictions posed by more conventional research enables communities to get you closer to your customers.

With regard to patient communities, the American Medical Association (AMA), based on reports by the Pricewaterhouse Cooper's Health Research Institute and from the Computer Sciences Corporation's (CSC) Global Institute for Emerging Healthcare Practices, identified that they are a good place for physicians to find out more information about topics patients are interested in, and thus what is important to their clients. In fact, opinions on social media sites about pharmaceuticals and therapies, healthcare services, and experiences is a valued source of information. Furthermore, having instant access to a global community of peers easily available to consult with (that is, PatientsLikeMe) provides numerous and invaluable benefits.

Apparently the debate about whether the medical community is prepared to embrace social media as an important tool for sharing medical information and delivering high-quality care to patients is, basically, over.

The main focus will now be on identifying the most effective ways to support the practical use of physician and patient communities, guaranteeing the information provided is reliable and targeting the right audience.

One of the most excellent examples of POC development and management is at the basis of the online qualitative research launched by a healthcare foundation, the Crohn's and Colitis Foundation of Canada (CCFC) in order to shift its focus (Hancock, 2012).[6] For several years, in fact, the CCFC focused entirely on discovering a cure. Fundraising efforts to help fund research had always been a priority over disease education and patient assistance. Nevertheless, with an increasing number of patient requests for information and assistance, the Foundation sought to find the main patient needs and opportunities to differentiate. The qualitative research approach, developed, and implemented by the qualitative researcher Layla Shea, focused on making it easy for Crohn's and Colitis patients to participate. She opted for an online method for two main reasons:

- *Sensitivity to patient needs*: Patients' difficulty to be away from home for even a few and social pressure resulting from discussing such a personal topic in a face-to-face setting.

- *Geographic reach*: Conducting online research allowed, in a single study, the involvement of respondents throughout the very large area served by CCFC. The research was planned to last ten days and included two activities each day:
  - *One poll*: the daily question "was today a good day or bad day and why?"
  - *One engagement activity*: Shea's activity-based conversations stimulated more discussion and personal interaction than a standard set of questions.

Activities aimed to allow participants to interact, share ideas, and offer support. For example, the "Let's Vent" activity requested participants to post about their frustrations. They were encouraged to write about things that irritate them or post photos or videos that described how they felt. This activity generated a lively conversation among respondents, who instantly began building on each others' posts and stories.

Findings from the research helped identify three specific stages of Crohn's and colitis diagnoses and the needs associated with those stages:

1.   Pre-diagnosis—"What's wrong with me?" The information needed while symptoms occur before a diagnosis is made.

2.   At diagnosis—"Help me understand." The desire for more information about how the patient's life will be affected and what they need to manage the disease.

3.   Post-diagnosis—"Help me take control." How can a patient create a meaningful life while managing this disease?

As a result, the CCFC created three specific communication strategies, tailoring tactics and messaging to the distinct needs and feelings of patients in each stage. In addition, it used the findings to realign its communication and education materials with the needs of both patients and HCPs.

The research truly helped the CCFC, which registered an increasing trend in the number of inquiries for information after the implementation of the new communication. There has also been a significant increase in the number of people attending CCFC conferences and educational events, as well as an increase in participation and donations at its fundraising events.

Even more importantly, the research is helping Crohn's and colitis patients satisfy their own specific needs and also benefit from the pleasure of helping others whose situations are similar to their own.

As the CCFC example shows, for a POC to develop into a long-term resource for an organization, it is crucial to get the right establishment and management of it.

Setting up and managing a POC from scratch can be an intimidating process, so it's suggested to break it down into the following stages (Digital MR, 2012):[7]

- Define the Scope

    a)   Size of the community

    b)   Specific objectives and target members

    c)   Customization.

- Recruit Members

    a)   Use appropriate resources and channels to recruit members

    b)   Appoint an Online Community Manager (OCM).

- Engage Members

  a)   Connect with members before starting activities

  b)   Talk to members from the first day they join

  c)   Connect them with each other

  d)   Plan activities for the duration of the research.

- Manage Activities

  a)   Execute research activities

  b)   Encourage co-creation

  c)   Reward participants when and how appropriate.

  d)   Share results

- Replenish Members

  a)   The OCM will minimize members attrition

  b)   Some members will inevitably drop out

  c)   Define a replenishment cycle.

Online Focus Groups

Different market research managers mean different things when they talk about online focus groups (Digital MR, 2012).[8] There are two main forms of focus group: synchronous or asynchronous.

- *Synchronous*: All participants are online at the same time.

- *Asynchronous*: The focus group members participate in the conversation when they are online.

Synchronous focus groups can be divided in four main forms:

1.   Virtual Focus Group

      This form involves six to eight participants who are online at the
      same time using video and audio to communicate with each other
      and with the moderator. Duration 60–90 minutes.

2.   Chat Group

      The six to eight participants communicate with each other and
      with the moderator by typing in a chat box. No video or audio is
      used. Duration 60–90 minutes.

3.   Enhanced Chat Group

      This is the same as the Chat Group for the participants the only
      difference is that the moderator alone uses video and audio.

4.   Mini Group

      This can take the form of any of the first three types described
      above with the only difference that there are fewer participants,
      that is, four to five.

Asynchronous focus groups can be divided in two main forms:

1.   Bulletin Board.

      This form involves 10–20 participants who participate when they
      are online by typing their responses to moderator questions that
      are posted in advance. This discussion may last from four to five
      days to a few weeks. Some call this a short-term community.

2.   Enhanced Bulletin Board.

      The same as a Bulletin Board but with the additional possibility
      for all to post photos or video clips in addition to their
      typed comments.

Other online qualitative research forms that do not fall under the description of focus groups in our view are:

- online in-depth interviews using chat or video and audio;

- online diaries;

- video or photo diaries;

- online diads and triads.

The main difference that focus group discussions (FGDs) have over the above methods is that more than four people are leading a discussion about a subject whereas the above are mainly one-to-one discussions.

CHOOSING THE RIGHT FORM OF FOCUS GROUP DISCUSSION

Choosing the most appropriate FGD is at the basis of the value and insightfulness of the findings you will get. It depends on the kind of topic (that is, sensitive), the level of needed interaction, and the importance of influence among participants. Table 3.1 lists some general guidelines on how to choose the appropriate form or method for your project:

Table 3.2   Appropriate form of focus group projects

IN DEPTH INTERVIEWS (IDIs) OR DIARIES

If the subject is sensitive or if we do not want the participants to be influenced by what other people say or show

VIRTUAL FOCUS GROUPS OR CHAT GROUPS

If the subject requires a more dynamic discussion with more interaction among the participants

SIMPLE CHAT GROUPS OR BULLETIN BOARDS

If participants are not very technologically savvy

ASYNCHRONOUS METHODS

For very low incidence and difficult to find participants

Choosing the most appropriate FGD is at the basis of the value and insightfulness of the findings you will get.

RECRUITMENT

Recruitment for online focus groups is a little different than for face-to-face ones. The traditional way is to go to a qualitative recruitment agency, provide the profile, agree on the incentive and then wait for the group participants to arrive on the set date. Recruitment can be done through consumer panels but this affects the quality of respondents: panelists may participate in surveys purely for the incentives and do whatever it takes to qualify for a research project. Another consideration is that some participants have great difficulties with the technology, even after coaching on the phone they are still challenged. This is why the software has to be very intuitive and very simple.

MODERATOR

If you are an end user of market research you probably already know the importance of the moderator. This is the person who will write the discussion guide based on your objectives, facilitate the discussion and write the report. A moderator will ideally be an experienced qualitative researcher. Academic disciplines that offer themselves for this job are Psychology and Sociology but they are not a pre-condition for a good moderator. There are certain moderating techniques (such as Projective Techniques) that are suitable for certain objectives and the moderator has to know when to use these methods.

INSIGHTS

Sometimes focus groups are used as a pre-cursor to a quantitative survey in order to provide support in the questionnaire design and sometimes they are the only research that will need to meet certain marketing objectives. The data can be available to the researcher as audio or video files, as a transcript of the discussion and uploaded images or video clips. In order for the researcher to be in a position to deliver valuable customer insights, they need to have a thorough understanding of the research objectives. These objectives need to be designed to be action oriented so that the insights in the research report will lead to actions that will in turn lead to a business benefit.

Focus on what matters to the patient

Notes

_1_ Kotler, P. and Armstrong G. (2014), _Principles of Marketing_, 15th edition. Harlow: Pearson Education, pp. 122–148.

_2_ Baym, N.K. (2007), The New Shape Of Online Community: The Example Of Swedish Independent Music Fandom. _First Monday_, 12(8) [online]. Available at http://firstmonday.org/ojs/index.php/fm/article/view/1978/1853 [Accessed 22 December 2014].

_3_ Di Mauro, V. Online Community Decision: Public, Private or Hybrid? [online]. Available at http://www.leadernetworks.com/2012/01/online-community-decision-public.html [Accessed 22 December 2014].

_4_ Digital MR (2012), How To Benefit From Private Online Communities (POCs). Integral reproduction.

_5_ Elsevier Health Sciences (2012), Social media—General Practitioners and Medical Specialists—Spain, UK, Germany, Brazil, Italy and France.

_6_ Hancock, K. (2012), Redefining the Message. Online Qual Guides Health Care Foundation to Shift its Focus. _Quirk's Marketing Resarch Review,_ Volume XXVI, No 10: 30–32.

_7_ Digital MR (2012), How To Benefit From Private Online Communities (POCs). Integral reproduction with permission.

_8_ Digital MR (2012), How To Make Online Focus Groups Work For You. Integral reproduction with permission.

Chapter 4

The Emergence of Online Opinion Leaders

JOHN MACK

Business network

The Internet and social media have spawned a new breed of trusted experts who other people look to for answers to their questions and advice about products. Many people would not dream of buying something online without first reading the comments from other purchasers. Amazon and other ecommerce sites also rank the usefulness of these opinions. Thus is created online "opinion leaders."

Jack Barrette, former pharmaceutical category leader at Yahoo! and currently CEO of WEGO Health, claims he coined the term consumer opinion leaders (COLs) to describe ordinary people who influence what many other consumers believe and buy. He cited examples from Yahoo! Answers, which is a social network where people ask questions and Yahoo! experts—who can be any qualified person—provide answers.

Other pundits have spoken about these kinds of people. For example, Malcom Gladwell—author of the book *The Tipping Point*—calls these people "mavens." "There is something about the personal, disinterested, expert opinion of a maven that makes us sit up and listen," says Gladwell.

The healthcare industry, including hospitals, insurers, medical device companies, and pharmaceutical companies also employ online opinion leaders in their marketing communications programs.

In this chapter, we first focus on how healthcare marketers have traditionally employed physician opinion leaders and how the digital world has changed the criteria for identifying these medical "mavens." Then we discuss the phenomenon of the online patient opinion leader (POL) as a special case of COL.

Key Physician Opinion Leaders

The number of factors influencing physician prescribing decisions and their communications with patients continues to grow, including clinical experience, journal articles, continuing medical education (CME) activity, managed care, detailing, events, journal advertising, patient requests, online information seeking, and so on. One of the most impactful influences on physicians has remained consistent: national, regional and/or local KOLs hired by pharmaceutical companies.

KOLs provide benefits to drug companies throughout the product lifecycle. In the research and development preclinical phase, KOLs identify gaps in medical information, offer valuable insights into disease states and patient treatment regimens, and help shape product development. During the clinical trial phase, KOLs help design and conduct clinical trials, and publish study results in peer-reviewed journals. In the commercialization and marketing phase, KOLs serve as product champions, give lectures to physicians, and help develop marketing strategies. Studies suggest that the largest pharmaceutical companies spend nearly a third of their total marketing expenditures for new products on KOLs.

Attributes of Physician Thought Leaders

Pharma companies that excel at building relationships with key opinion leading physicians open doors that enable them to disseminate new product information and clinical trial results to the medical community through trusted sources. Without the KOLs to legitimize claims made by sales reps, the sales rep return on investment might be much less than it is, whatever the exact number may be. Although physicians are more interested in true thought leaders who have credentials such as academic standing and/or have performed clinical trials, some KOLs are chosen more for their high prescribing habits than for their knowledge or other attribute that would enable them to influence their peers.

Key Opinion Leaders provide benefits to drug companies throughout the product lifecycle.

As uncertainty increases—for example, when a new drug is launched and there is not a lot of definitive clinical information—doctors rely more heavily on the advice or opinions of respected peers. A successful KOL strategy must first discover who these influential doctors are, have a ranking process, and finally have strategies to engage and develop relationships with them. Strengthening corporate reputation with this customer segment will greatly impact business success. Companies can also use reputation tracking as a measure for evaluating the overall effectiveness of influential physician development programs.

Methods of identifying influential KOLs include:

- bibliometrics—secondary research and evaluation of publications, conference participation, roles on committees or in organizations, industry affiliations (are they associated with other companies? What clinical trials are they a part of?), and so on;

- peer nomination/sociometric;

- claims/referral data analysis.

Each method has pros and cons. Bibliometrics, for example, is fairly inexpensive but will capture a limited number of physicians, mostly weighted toward researchers and academics. Peer nomination is essentially a very large survey asking doctors whom they rely on for advice. It generates very granular data but involves a fairly significant investment, the size of which is a function of the size of the audience being studied. Turnaround is months given the time needed for fieldwork as well as data processing.

Gary Bartolacci, Senior Director, Kantar Health, cited research that questioned the traditional idea of thought leaders being perceived and defined by prestigious titles, number of publications, and speaking engagements.[1] Other physicians may not fit that definition but are nevertheless quite influential—especially at the local and regional levels. Some attributes of influential doctors identified by this research include:

- good listeners;

- clinically competent;

- caring;

- technically competent;

- socially accessible;

- conformity to the system norms.

"Accessibility is a very important one," said Bartolacci. "How accessible is a national KOL going to be to a community doctor with a question about a particular patient? Probably not that accessible." Batolacci advises that, when using a KOL for a speaker program, make sure that their standard of practice conforms with that of the audience.

Once you have identified these influential physicians, you are going to need to develop some way to rank them. Scores can be developed on various metrics. The various fields researched in a bibliometric approach, for example, can give multiple metrics—volumes of publications, media mentions, presentations given, committee and guideline involvement, and so on.

Without the KOLs to legitimize claims made by sales reps, the sales rep return on investment might be much less than it is, whatever the exact number may be.

The Power of Peer Influence

Peer nomination and/or claims data analysis can each independently give very good metrics for ranking. Experts stress the importance to normalize each of the metrics, which will allow weighting in the development of an overall score. But don't rely too heavily on an overall rank for doctors. A doctor in a peer nomination study, for example, may be mentioned by only one other doctor, but that doctor may happen to be the most heavily mentioned doctor in the study. Using an overall score may cause that doctor to be overlooked.

Peer influence is amplified when there is uncertainty and a lack of definitive clinical information (in other words, when conditions are ripe for seeking advice). Research has shown that these interpersonal communications are especially critical when physicians are forming opinions about and deciding whether to adopt or reject a new therapy.

Online Physician Key Opinion Leaders

Research sponsored by Pfizer and published in 2012 in the *Journal of Medical Internet Research*,[2] found that over 70 percent of physicians surveyed (N=485) are either "current users" (52 percent) or "likely/very likely" users (19 percent) of "restricted online communities" (such as Sermo). In this case, "use" means sharing medical information and staying up to date professionally.

Peer influence is amplified when there is uncertainty and a lack of definitive clinical information (in other words, when conditions are ripe for seeking advice).

These days, many influential physicians are found in closed online communities and pharmaceutical companies are actively seeking them out (see, for example, Sermo Case Study, below). "There may be newer doctors who are incredibly influential on social media sites who are not considered key opinion leaders in the real world or who are completely unknown to companies," noted Bartolacci. With the growing importance of social media, the impact just one of these influential doctors or KOLs can have is significant, particularly if they are actively blogging about their satisfaction or dissatisfaction with your company. "The power of one person is greatly enhanced with these new technologies … it may be a good idea to incorporate social media in your overall KOL strategy," said Bartolacci.

COLLABORATING WITH ONLINE PHYSICIAN COMMUNITIES

Pharma–Physician Peer-to-Peer Dialogue via Sermo

On October 15, 2007, Pfizer and Sermo—a Web-based community currently comprised of 270,000 US physicians in the US and now part of WorldOne's Global Networked Community comprising over 1.8 million HCPs spanning 80 countries—announced a "strategic collaboration designed to redefine the way physicians in the US and the healthcare industry work together to improve patient care."

Through this collaboration, Sermo's community of 35,000 physicians had access to Pfizer's clinical content in tangible ways that allow for the transparent and efficient exchange of knowledge. With access to the most comprehensive and up-to-date information on Pfizer products, says Sermo, physicians will be able to find the data they need, when they need it, to make informed decisions.

On the opposite side of the coin, Pfizer will have access to Sermo's physicians and online discussions. There are three ways that clients such as Pfizer can interact with Sermo members:

- Observe ("AlphaMD"): AlphaMD serves as a sort of "radar screen" through which clients can view Sermo's community, by creating a customized watch list to track subjects based on keyword tags (for example, product names).

- Insight: Clients can gain insight by posting questions on Sermo and getting replies from physicians, including poll data. The idea is to mine the "wisdom of the crowd."

- Action ("HotSpots"): The HotSpots technology allows pharmaceutical clients to insert icons next to targeted topics that physicians can click on to access information or offers (for example, samples) from clients. Upon clicking the Hotspot icon, a pop-up invitation appears and the physician can follow the links out of Sermo onto the client's site to retrieve the information or offer. Clients can create and monitor their own HotSpots without requiring intervention from Sermo.

Pfizer claimed its aim was to pursue the following objectives through its collaboration with Sermo:

- discover, with physicians, how best to transform the way medical information is exchanged in the fast-moving social media environment;

- create an open and transparent discussion with physicians through the innovative channel offered by online exchange;

- engage with the FDA to define guidelines for the use of social media in communications with HCPs;

- work with physicians to develop a productive exchange between pharmaceutical professionals and the Sermo community.

It's also possible Pfizer used Sermo's HotSpot feature to recruit doctors to influence other doctors. By monitoring and engaging in Sermo conversations, Pfizer can learn the following:

- which doctors on Sermo are its friends;

- which ones have the highest ratings among other Sermo doctors and therefore are likely to be influential; and

- which doctors seem interested in becoming consultants or doing clinical trials.

"Peer nomination" is an important method of identifying online physician opinion leaders. Because online peer nomination is an automatic function of most physician discussion forums such as Sermo, it is instantaneous and constantly updated. Keep in mind, however, that physicians on Sermo and other sites have complete and final control over their online identities—they decide who will be able to see any identifiable information about them.

Traditionally, thought leaders have always been medical society and academic-based physicians. "Yet," said Daniel Palestrant, MD, founder and former CEO of Sermo, "there is more and more of a chasm between these types of leaders and the physicians in the trenches treating patients. The world-views and priorities of these two groups are divergent. What's intriguing to me is this entirely new generation of opinion leaders developing on Sermo. Their views are not the same as academics. They have a far less esoteric and more pragmatic view on how to treat patients. For example, reimbursement for treatment may be a more important issue for practicing physicians than academic-based physicians. Everyone agrees on the science, but the question is how to translate this into action to help patients."[3]

"Peer nomination" is an important method of identifying online physician opinion leaders.

Will Online Information Replace Peer-Reviewed Journals?

Many online physician communities, such as DocCheck in Germany, post medical content that rivals the content in peer-reviewed medical journals, according to DocCheck President, Frank Antwerpes, MD. A DocCheck 2010 survey suggested that a substantial portion—23 percent—of physicians who use the network also post content, while 67 percent just read content.[4]

The DocCheck survey also asked why doctors post information on medical websites. The responses were as follows:

- 60 percent said: To get help from my colleagues regarding a medical issue I am dealing with.

- 56 percent said: To share information I receive from other sources.

- 40 percent said: To share techniques I have developed or insights I have learned with my colleagues.

- 11 percent said: Other reasons (for example, to state my opinion, to correct facts).

"Given a very active community of physicians contributing content," said Dr. Antwerpes, "maybe there will a paradigm shift in the medical communications market that reduces the role of traditional key opinion leaders with a shift to what I call 'community opinion leader.' Such an opinion leader earns his or her status not because of a stellar academic career, but by virtue of a social media career."

More than 60 percent of respondents to the DocCheck survey agreed that some day online physician-generated content may replace or be as important as peer-reviewed journals. "The idea that the Web can change the rules of classical opinion making in medicine is quite acceptable to physicians, who see from their own experience that the game is changing," said Dr. Antwerpes.

Online Patient Opinion Leaders

Drug companies and hospitals have long used celebrities to endorse their products. However, some market research shows that the sick are relying more on the recommendations of fellow patients, and less on the reputations of companies and endorsers, in deciding whether to seek treatment and what drugs to ask for. Patient "ambassadors," for example, have long been used by the healthcare industry to share their personal experiences with prospective patients and to provide inspiration to others like them who are battling the same medical condition.

Portraying patients and patient stories in healthcare advertising is a growing phenomenon, which is being closely monitored by researchers. A recent study of US cancer center TV and magazine ads, for example, found that these ads, many of which feature real patients or actors portraying patients (often it's difficult to tell one from the other), rely heavily on emotional appeal and only lightly touch on facts that patients need to know. The study was published online in the *Annals of Internal Medicine* in May 2014.

Online patient discussion boards and other social media have made it easy for patient advocates to tell their stories and gain recognition as credible sources of information. Pharmaceutical companies have taken note of this and have solicited patient stories via unbranded social media sites such as J&J Lifescan's Diabetes Handprint, a website that encourages each visitor to write a word on his or her hand expressing their feelings about diabetes, and sharing the story behind it. Users were able to click on the "Sharing" button to see "Real Stories" of people with diabetes. Although these "Real Stories" may have been authentic, they were not UGC, which is the hallmark of social media.

Portraying patients and patient stories in healthcare advertising is a growing phenomenon ...

These days, healthcare marketers are using real patients in their direct-to-consumer (DTC) TV and print ads and pharmaceutical companies are soliciting real patient stories on their websites, YouTube channels and Facebook pages. In this era of the e-Patient—a new breed of informed health consumer who uses the Internet to gather health information—some patients are becoming POLs who are recruited by pharmaceutical and other healthcare companies in a similar fashion to physician KOLs. These COLs or POLs influence other patients through social media such as blogs, Twitter, and Facebook and at industry-sponsored gatherings.

POLs may be pharma's "secret sauce" for social media marketing because they have the benefit of already being part of the "conversation," which neatly solves the marketer's problem of how to "join the conversation." POLs are valued based on their reputations within leading online patient social networks, participation in national patient advocacy organizations, membership of special POL networks such as WEGO Health, tweeting and blog posting metrics (number of followers, readers, etc.), and even participation in clinical trials.

DIABETES OPINION LEADERS PAID BY ROCHE TO CURATE CONTENT ON NEW TWITTER-BASED SOCIAL MEDIA SITE

Diabetes Nest, according to its "About" statement, was "a Twitter-based diabetes network designed to help people discover the best conversations from the most meaningful voices. The Nest was created by Ignite Health and sponsored by Roche Diabetes Care, makers of ACCU-CHEK® products and services."

Ignite Health, formerly part of the InVentiv Health agency, maintained the site. Fabio Gratton, former Chief Experience Officer at Ignite Health, said:

"Few argue that social media has transformed how patients and their caregivers share healthcare information and find support. But the sheer volume of content can be overwhelming."

"So we asked ourselves how we could best help the diabetes community find and engage in the most timely, relevant and important conversations. The result is a simple, intuitive, compelling and ultimately self-sustaining diabetes social media community."

Diabetes Nest aggregates, sorts and ranks tweets from a curated list of diabetes experts.

All five of those "diabetes experts" were long-time patient bloggers who were "compensated for their time, effort and invaluable guidance." Caretakers included:

- Amy Tenderich (Diabetes Mine blogger)
- Gina Capone ("gina—your diabetes BFF" blogger)
- Kerri Sparling ("six until me" blogger)
- George Simmons (co-host of DSMA Live on BlogTalkRadio)
- Scott K. Johnson (co-host of DSMA Live on BlogTalkRadio and blogger at Scott's Diabetes)

Roche claimed to have "no control or influence over the content or frequency of the Caretakers' tweets."

Diabetes Nest is the first time that bloggers have been paid to be "consumer/patient opinion leaders" in a manner similar to how pharma often pays physicians to be "key opinion leaders."

Online patient discussion boards and other social media have made it easy for patient advocates to tell their stories and gain recognition as credible sources of information.

Patient Opinion Leaders are the New Key Opinion Leaders

As it becomes more and more difficult for healthcare industry sales people to gain access to physicians online and off, these companies will leverage consumers and patients to promote their products, especially via social media. POLs may one day replace physician KOLs altogether!

At a patient panel discussion during a 2010 industry conference, Allison Blass—a patient blogger and diabetes activist—told the audience about attending a "Diabetes Social Media Summit" sponsored by Roche in Orlando, Florida. Allison came away from that Summit feeling much closer to Roche and now has a more personal relationship with "Todd," one of the Roche Summit organizers who was communicating with Allison before the event. "Oh my God," said Allison at the Summit, "I'm finally getting to meet you!"

The physicians' ears next door were probably burning with envy. They probably miss the good old days when pharma companies could invite THEM to outings at resort locations. But that's now forbidden by the US industry's trade group (PhRMA) in its voluntary Code on Interactions With Health Care Professionals. There are no PhRMA guidelines, however, about hiring and paying "patient self advocates" to attend "summits" at resort locations.

At that same conference, Blass said, "You need to pay some one's full time salary," referring to the desire of some pharma companies to interact with patients in online communities. "The only way to sustain growth and involvement in a [online] community," said Blass, "is to have someone who actually does it [manage social media interactions with patients] as their job … to become the person who is known and loved by the community."[5]

Not that there is anything wrong with being compensated for your time, but pharmaceutical companies have to be careful how they provide compensation. Just like physicians, patients are human and susceptible to the influences of flattery and rewards.

In the case of Diabetes Nest, Roche probably supplies an "unrestricted grant," which is supposed to specify that the grantor (Roche) has no control over the content created by the grantee.

The "grantee" in this case was probably Ignite Health, which owned Diabetes Nest. Ignite Health at the time was an advertising agency that worked with pharmaceutical companies.

A pharmaceutical company providing unrestricted grants or other funds to an advertising agency in support of a patient site related to a product line is a bit controversial, especially if the lines between the funding and advertising interests are blurred.

This kind of thing got pharma companies into trouble with US Senator Grassley when "unrestricted grants" were provided to ad agencies to run so-called "independent" accredited CME programs for physicians. The Accreditation Council for Continuing Medical Education (ACCME), which accredits CME in the US, now requires CME providers to be independent of ad agencies to avoid conflicts of interest. Perhaps this should also be the best practice for grants given in support of POL educational projects such as Diabetes Nest.

The main issue is "transparency," which may be a new concept for eager patient advocates who wish to be hired as pharma POLs.

The US Federal Trade Commission (FTC) is well aware of the potential abuse of using POLs as paid industry spokespeople. In 2013, the FTC revised its Guides Concerning the Use of Endorsements and Testimonials in Advertising,[6] which address endorsements by consumers, experts, organizations, and celebrities, as well as the disclosure of important connections between advertisers and endorsers. The revised Guides added new examples to illustrate the long-standing principle that "material connections" (sometimes payments or free products) between advertisers and endorsers—connections that consumers would not expect—must be disclosed. These examples address what constitutes an endorsement when the message is conveyed by bloggers or other word of mouth (WOM) marketers. And advertisements that feature a consumer and convey his or her experience with a product or service as typical when that is not the case will be required to clearly disclose the results that consumers can generally expect.

Specifically regarding the health industry, Jim Zuffoletti, President of openQ, predicted in a pharmaceutical industry conference presentation that "social media driven patient advocates or Patient Opinion Leaders will receive significant scrutiny" by the HHS's Office of Inspector General (OIG).

What best practices should govern pharma's collaboration with POLs? Should the industry develop guidelines for their interactions with POLs via social networks (for example, develop a "Patient Opinion Leader Transparency Policy")?

An online survey[7] of *Pharma Marketing News* readers asked whether or not they agreed or disagreed with the following statements related to Possible POL "Best Practices" Scenarios:

1. Pharma companies should be free to hire knowledgeable patients to ENGAGE (carry on discussions) with patients within online PATIENT discussion forums that the company owns or sponsors.

2. Pharma companies should be free to hire knowledgeable patients to MODERATE online PATIENT discussion forums that the company owns or sponsors.

3. Pharma companies should be free to hire knowledgeable patients to ENGAGE with healthcare providers (HCPs) on online HCP discussion forums that the company owns or sponsors.

4.   Pharma companies should be free to hire knowledgeable patients to post messages to and engage in conversation in independent online patient forums.

5.   Patients who participate in online health forums should reveal their financial dealings with pharma companies—for example, money, gifts, or other benefits such as all expenses paid trips—much like physician authors do in medical journals.

6.   Pharma interactions and communications with POLs are subject to FDA laws and regulations governing promotion of prescription drugs.

7.   Every pharmaceutical company should have a "POL Transparency Policy" that details the nature of its financial dealings with patients who participate in online health forums.

The results are summarized in the chart shown in Figure 4.1.

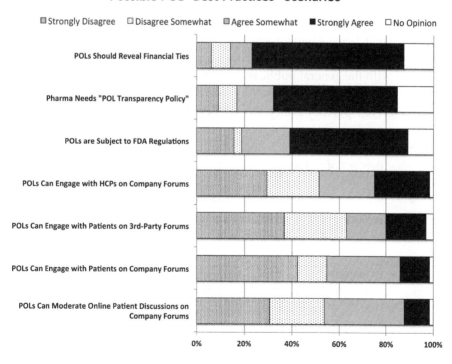

Possible POL "Best Practices" Scenarios

Figure 4.1   Survey responses to Possible POL "Best Practices" Scenarios

Source: Pharma Marketing News.

Patient Opinion Leaders Transparency and Policies

There was strong support among respondents for transparency in terms of revealing financial ties and making sure that pharma companies have a publicly available policy outlining their POL terms of employment. While creating and promoting POLs is a good idea, the key word here is knowledgeable. This would mean that the company provides adequate information on its products but does not incentivize the POL to influence or drive patients toward usage of the company's products. "Health netizens," said one respondent, "are looking for balanced information online and that's what a POL must provide in order to become a POL and gain online credibility." In light of the burgeoning empowerment of patients and desire to participate more actively, "patients should be able to work directly with pharma, not necessarily to promote drugs or agents but do consult to insure that messaging and advertising are done with patient needs first," said another respondent.

Of course, credibility amongst peers is the most important qualification for hiring POLs (and KOLs) in the first place. This was emphasized by another respondent: "The educational and professional qualifications of POLs should also influence if/how they are hired and engaged. Appropriate qualifications that go beyond 'being a patient and an advocate' should be established and met prior to inception." Obviously, the hiring of patients who are not "qualified" as "experts" with the general public should be avoided.

Every POL Transparency Policy should include:

- activities for which the pharma company pays their POLs (83 percent of survey respondents agree);

- how the pharma company ensures that laws and industry policies regarding financial relations with patients are followed (83 percent of survey respondents agree);

- explanation of why the pharma company collaborates with patients/ POLs (79 percent of survey respondents agree);

- how the pharma company selects POLs; that is, what qualifications are required (69 percent of survey respondents agree);

- what kind of training, if any, the pharma company provides to its POLs (68 percent of survey respondents agree).

There are several ways to make the policy accessible to the public, including:

- The policy should be easily accessible by the public via poduct.com websites as well as the corporate website.

- A link to the policy should be prominently placed within each online patient community where pharma patient collaborators are engaged in posting messages, joining discussions and/or managing discussions.

- Every pharma patient collaborator covered by the policy should reveal his or her relationship with the pharma company and provide a link to the policy. This could be done in the signature line or about tagline.

Respondents strongly supported the need for FDA regulation of POLs hired by pharmaceutical companies. In fact, social media guidelines published in January, 2014, by the FDA addresses how it will regulate "agents" speaking on behalf of drug and medical device companies. In this guidance,[8] the FDA says that "a firm is responsible for UGC [User-Generated Content] and communications of its employees or anyone acting on behalf of the firm and, as such, those materials are subject to submission to FDA to meet the postmarketing submission requirements." This directly applies to COLs hired by pharmaceutical companies.

In addition the FDA says: "FDA will not ordinarily view UGC on firm-owned or firm-controlled venues such as blogs, message boards, and chat rooms as promotional content on behalf of the firm as long as the user has no affiliation with the firm and the firm had no influence on the UGC."

The Nebulousness of "Influence"

In comments to the FDA, PhRMA contested the meaning of "influence" in this and in subsequent draft guidances from the FDA:

> *While a firm should be responsible for comments by an employee, agent, advisor, or paid speaker acting on behalf of the firm, the Final Guidance should clarify that such agents may be speaking on their own behalf, in which case their content should be treated as independent of a manufacturer. For example, some paid speakers may be experts*

in therapeutic areas [for example, KOLs], and although a firm might engage a speaker to speak on the firm's behalf on occasion, the individual may make statements in social media without the firm's knowledge or control. Similarly, a firm might engage with a third party, such as a consumer health advocate [for example, COL], to develop content for the firm-owned site. The health advocate may make statements in social media about her specific area of interest without the firm's knowledge or control. Likewise, a firm may maintain policies, training and education for employees about appropriate use of interactive social media. Nevertheless, that employee may act outside the scope of his employment and independently post information about a personal experience with a medicine or some other event without the firm's knowledge or control. Therefore, we suggest that FDA provide examples in the Final Guidance that illustrate when an employee, agent, or paid speaker is not acting on behalf of or prompted by the firm. The firm should be responsible only for statements that it actually causes or controls. As previously discussed, it would be inappropriate to hold a firm responsible for independently generated statements—even from individuals with whom the firm has a financial or other relationship—if the firm did not cause or control the content.[9]

The Celebrity Patient Opinion Leader

As noted previously, there are no PhRMA guidelines about hiring and paying "patient self advocates;" that is, POLs. Thus, pharmaceutical companies are free to pay well-respected patient members of social networks to speak glowingly about their products in online conversations. However, PhRMA's "Guiding Principles for Direct to Consumer (DTC) Advertisements About Prescription Medicines" does address the use of paid endorsements by celebrities. In the December, 2008 revision, this principle (#11) was added:

Where a DTC television or print advertisement features a celebrity endorser, the endorsements should accurately reflect the opinions, findings, beliefs or experience of the endorser. Companies should maintain verification of the basis of any actual or implied endorsements made by the celebrity endorser in the DTC advertisement, including whether the endorser is or has been a user of the product if applicable.[10]

Such celebrities have long been featured in offline drug ads in magazines and on TV. These days, some celebrities act just like patient advocates and can be considered a special class of POLs employed by the healthcare industry, including pharmaceutical companies. An example is actress, singer, and NFL wife, Holly Elizabeth Robinson Peete who is featured as part of Shire's "Keep Momming" campaign, which seeks to help mothers better identify the symptoms of Attention Deficit Hyperactivity Disorder (ADHD) in young girls. Peete's daughter, who has ADHD, is also featured in the campaign.

They tell their story in a video on Shire's KeepMomming.com website, the title of which is "Real Stories from Real Moms & Daughters." The search engine friendly metadata tag line is: "Find information on ADHD in children, as well as an ADHD symptom checklist, then talk to the doctor."

... some celebrities act just like patient advocates and can be considered a special class of POLs ...

Celebrity Patient Video Testimonials are Persuasive

There's plenty of information about ADHD on the site and the videos on the home page reel visitors in like fish attracted to the bait. All this "patient education" panders to the "e-patient"—the new breed of informed health consumers, using the Internet to gather information about a medical condition of particular interest to them. E-patients should be wary about the bait and be sure to gather information from a number of online sources before asking their doctors for a particular treatment.

To help answer the many questions that are raised by using real patient testimonials, including celebrity patient video testimonials, *Pharma Marketing News* hosted an online survey[11] that asked respondents' opinions. Survey respondents were asked to evaluate the following claims regarding patient testimonial ads:

- depending on the condition, these ads are more likely to motivate viewers to visit a doctor (71 percent of survey respondents agree);

- these ads are more believable (62 percent of survey respondents agree);

- these ads are more memorable (57 percent of survey respondents agree);

- these ads are more likely to gain attention and cut through the "clutter" (55 percent of survey respondents agree);

- patient-endorsed brands are seen as having less dangerous side effects than similar drugs (53 percent of survey respondents agree);

- patient-endorsed brands are seen as more effective than similar drugs (51 percent of survey respondents agree).

Overstating Efficacy

When pharma companies disseminate branded patient testimonial videos via the Internet—especially those videos featuring celebrity patients—the videos overstate the efficacy of drug treatment more often than other kinds of promotions according to an analysis of FDA warning letters (WLs) by Mark Senak, author of Eye On FDA Blog.[12] Senak analyzed 235 WLs and Notice of Violation (NOVs) letters issued by FDA's Office of Pharmaceutical Drug Promotion (OPDP) since 2005. He cataloged 600 violations, including:

- risk omission or minimization;

- superiority claims;

- overstatement of efficacy;

- unsubstantiated claims; and

- broadening of indication.

When Senak specifically looked at letters regarding pharma marketing videos (excluding TV DTC ad videos), he found that 80 percent of the violations concerned risk minimization (40 percent) or overstatement of efficacy (40 percent). These data are summarized in the chart in Figure 4.2.

What's interesting is that these videos—mostly patient and physician testimonials—overstate efficacy at TWICE the average rate for all kinds of promotions (40 percent for videos vs. 21 percent for all ads, including video). Senak postulates that "when people talk about their own experiences with a treatment, [they] may include reference to outcomes that is not typical or supported by clinical data."

An example of a video that overstated efficacy was another online Shire video (on YouTube) testimonial featuring celebrity Ty Pennington. In a WL to

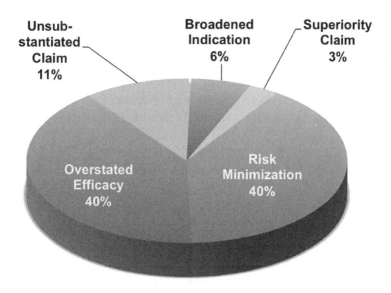

Figure 4.2   FDA cited violations for pharma videos
Source: Pharma Marketing News.

Shire, the FDA said, "Both the webpage and video overstate the efficacy of Adderall XR; the video also omits important information regarding the risks associated with Adderall XR use."

e-Patient Beware

According to the results of two separate social media-related studies unveiled at the American College of Gastroenterology's (ACG) 76th Annual Scientific meeting in Washington, DC, social networking sites like Facebook and YouTube may be sources of misleading information that could potentially do more harm than good. According to researcher Saurabh Mukewar, MD, the author of "YouTube: A Friend or Foe When You Are Taking Care of IBD Patients:"

> *Clinicians and their patients need to be aware of misleading information posted by patients or particularly by pharmaceutical companies who often post videos to make it seem like they are coming from a patient when in actuality it is a company advertisement. These sources are not transparent.[13]*

Dr. Mukewar agrees that the Internet and social media can benefit patients and enhance their care. But Dr. Mukewar said his findings are concerning to him since irritable bowel disease (IBD) patients may get misleading information via YouTube that could be harmful to their health.

People struggling with a chronic illness are much more likely to engage with messaging that they feel is both authentic and realistic. Patient testimonials can be incredibly powerful, but it is imperative that the POLs—including celebrity POLs—present a balanced story that is typical of all patients.

Use spokespersons responsibly

Notes

1   Mack, J., Corporate Reputation in the New Media World, *Pharma Marketing News* [online]. Available at http://www.pharma-mkting.com/news/pmn91-article02.pdf [Accessed 9 January 2015].

2   McGowen, B.S., et al., Understanding the Factors That Influence the Adoption and Meaningful Use of Social Media by Physicians to Share Medical Information, *Journal of Medical Internet Research* [online]. Available at http://www.jmir.org/2012/5/e117/ [Accessed 9 January 2015].

3   Mack, J., Collaborating with Online Physician Communities, *Pharma Marketing News* [online]. Available at http://www.news.pharma-mkting.com/pmn69-article01.pdf [Accessed 9 January 2015].

4   Mack, J., Pharma Collaboration with Online Patient Opinion Leaders, *Pharma Marketing News* [online]. Available at http://www.news.pharma-mkting.com/ PMNews_99_Upfront.pdf [Accessed 9 January 2015].

5   Mack, J., Pharma Collaboration with Online Patient Opinion Leaders, *Pharma Marketing News* [online]. Available at http://www.news.pharma-mkting.com/ PMNews_99_Upfront.pdf [Accessed 9 January 2015].

6   Federal Trade Commission, Guides Concerning the Use of Endorsements and Testimonials in Advertising [online]. Available at http://www.ftc.gov/sites/default/ files/attachments/press-releases/ftc-publishes-final-guides-governing-endorsements-testimonials/091005revisedendorsementguides.pdf [Accessed 9 January 2015].

7   Mack, J., Should Pharma Hire Online "Patient Opinion Leaders"?, *Pharma Marketing News* [online]. Available at http://www.surveys.pharma-mkting.com/POL-Collab-survey.htm [Accessed 9 January 2015].

8   US Food and Drug Administration, Guidance for Industry Fulfilling Regulatory Requirements for Postmarketing Submissions of Interactive Promotional Media for Prescription Human and Animal Drugs and Biologics [online]. Available at http://www.fda.gov/downloads/drugs/guidancecomplianceregulatoryinformation/ guidances/ucm381352.pdf [Accessed 9 January 2015].

9   Pharmaguy, PhRMA Questions Legality of FDA's Recent Social Media Guidance, Pharma Marketing Blog [online]. Available at http://pharmamkting.blogspot. com/2014/04/phrma-questions-legality-of-fdas-recent.html [Accessed 9 January 2015].

10   PhRMA, Guiding Principles for Direct to Consumer (DTC) Advertisements About Prescription Medicines [online]. Available at http://www.phrma.org/sites/default/files/ pdf/phrmaguidingprinciplesdec08final.pdf [Accessed 9 January 2015].

11   Mack, J., Use of Patient Testimonials in DTC & Social Media Advertising Survey, *Pharma Marketing News* [online]. Available at http://www.surveys.pharma-mkting.com/ Pat-testimonial-survey.htm [Accessed 9 January 2015].

12   Senak, M., Some Digital and Social Media Guidance—FDA Regulation of Pharma Communications in a Digital Era—A White Paper, Fleishman Hillard [online]. Available at http://www.eyeonfda.com/eye_on_fda/2013/04/some-digital-and-social-media-guidance-fda-regulation-of-pharma-communications-in-a-digital-era-a-white-paper.html [Accessed 9 January 2015].

13   Mack, J., Online e-Patient & Celebrity Patient Video Testimonials, *Pharma Marketing News* [online]. Available at http://www.pharma-mkting.com/news/ pmnews1308-article01.pdf [Accessed 9 January 2015].

Chapter 5

Building a Winning Digital Communication Strategy for Patients

LETIZIA AFFINITO

At this point you have learned what health marketing communication is, how important understanding customers is, as well as effectively gathering and using customer insights.

You're now ready to look deeper into marketing comsmunication strategy and tactics. In this chapter we look further into key customer-driven marketing communication strategy decisions—dividing markets into meaningful customer groups (segmentation), choosing which customer groups to serve (targeting), creating communication initiatives and tools which best serve targeted customers (differentiation), and positioning them in the mind of patients (positioning).

When developing a patient-driven digital communication strategy you have to "stop demanding the web conform to your desire for mass—and instead realize that mattering a lot to a few people is worth far more than mattering just a little to everyone" (Godin, 2011).[1]

Because consumers talk about their passions and needs in online communities, understanding those conversations is a valuable resource for innovation and strategy development. Finding the hidden passion and/or need generated by online consumer segments is critical to the success of a patient-driven digital communication strategy.

Because consumers talk about their passions and needs in online communities, understanding those conversations is a valuable resource for innovation and strategy development.

Psychographic Segmentation Reveals Pockets of Passion and Needs

In the complex digital world of social media, content marketing, e-mail, reviews, and so on, health communicators need to find strategies to engage online users in specific actions, such as sharing content, recommending it to others, opening e-mails, writing reviews, and so on.

To encourage social media users to take these actions, you first have to understand what encourages them, which necessitates psychographic segmentation; that is, classifying people by their attitude and behavior. This form of social network psychographic segmentation is known as "socialgraphics," which catches the behavior, characteristic, attitude, and, most of all, motivations of customers online. Understanding an audience's "socialgraphics" allows communicators to design Internet marketing strategies which interest and maintains customers in different online settings.

Socialgraphics will help healthcare communicators in developing a winning value proposition, making digital communication content more valuable for the patient and launching more impactful patient-centered initiatives and tools.

A health-related socialgraphics analysis asks key questions such as: Where do patients and physicians go online? What kinds of social behavior are they engaged in? What information and kinds of people do they rely on? What's their social influence? Who trusts them? How does my intended audience use social media to engage with healthcare products and services? You will need to concentrate on the relationships, not on technologies.[2]

As we have seen in Chapter 3, you can understand your audience's sociographics through surveys, observational techniques, secondary search, or simply immersing yourself in different groups and platforms to understand what is going in each online venue. To help digital communicators analyze customer's evolving social behaviors and benefit from this evolution, Forrester has introduced the Social Technographics Score (2013),[3] a new model which focuses on commercial social behaviors, which, differently from many other surveys, is based on how audiences interact with and talk about companies, brands, and products. It also helps communicators choose among social strategies by measuring where in the customer lifecycle audiences are most likely to use social tools. It, basically, works in two stages:

1.   *The overall score tells you whether social is important to your marketing plan*: If your audience scores in the middle range—if they're "Social Savvies" or "Social Snackers"—social should serve as support tools within your marketing plans; if your audience scores low—"Social Skippers"—you should put as few resources into social media as possible.

2.   *The discover, explore, and engage factors which tell you where social is important to your plan.* Once you've decided how heavily social will feature in your marketing plan, you'll still need to know what types of social interactions your audiences are looking for.

Understanding an audience's "socialgraphics" allows communicators to design Internet marketing strategies which interest and maintains customers in different online settings.

Targeting the Right Audience

Once you have defined the segments you will need to profile them using all available data. Then you will have to choose which segment/segments better represent your targets.

You will have to execute the following main steps, mostly if you need insights to develop your social media strategy:

- Analyze the results to find out:

  - WHY customers are in the segment they are and why they buy the product/service or engage in the activity;
  - WHO they are;
  - HOW, WHEN and WHERE do they engage with the product category in question.

- Choose the ideal segment(s) to target based on size and value to the company but also easiness and cost to access and suitability of your offer.

- Develop a value proposition for each segment and by extension the Unique Selling Proposition, a brand promise and the positioning in general.

- Develop the engagement strategy for each segment in order to communicate the value the new proposition will bring, to stimulate further online engagement and Word of Mouth (WOM).

Online Needs-Based Customer Segmentation May Improve Your Social Media Strategy

The ultimate goal of any customer segmentation is to be able to easily identify prospects and leads and to place them in their respective segments in order to follow up with the right messaging and the right initiatives and tools for each lead. Social media has led to a profusion of sources for leads so responding to them in a systematic and cost effective way is key.

Once your segments are identified, named, and targeted, a possible next step is to place existing customers in their respective segments by asking them a few questions—ideally less than ten. According to M. Michael (Digital MR 2012),[4] social media gives marketers much greater access not just to larger samples, but also to samples that include groups of consumers who were previously difficult to identify or to recruit. One area where this is applicable, and relatively straightforward, is when a brand has a Facebook fan-page. They can invite customers to answer five to ten questions in order to pass them through a segmentation algorithm and categorize them accordingly.

Proper customer targeting with the appropriate messaging, (whether through traditional means, or as is increasingly the case, through social media) saves marketing money and delivers higher revenue overall and per customer.

This section lays out, in simple steps, how a needs-based customer segmentation should be conducted and utilized for maximum results.

SURVEY SAMPLE DEFINITION

The sample for the needs-based customer segmentation survey has to be defined as broadly as possible. Usually this entails a representative sample of product/service users or a nationally representative sample. For example, if your communication initiative or tool is related to a cancer drug or treatment (that is, radiotherapy) it doesn't make sense to include people without cancer and perhaps only include certain types of patients. Leveraging social media platforms such as Facebook can make accessing niche samples much easier. On the other hand if your communication initiative or tool is related to supplements, you may decide to go for a nationally representative sample, as the likelihood in finding interesting targets among a general demographic is relatively high.

> ## Once your segments are identified, named, and targeted, a possible next step is to place existing customers in their respective segments ...

An ideal sample size for this kind of survey is n=1000 but there are circumstances where a lower sample (down to n=500) will be effective. The challenge with the smaller sample sizes is not only that the standard error is larger but that we may miss an opportunity to identify a small high-value segment. It is advisable to use larger samples when we aim for national representation and smaller samples for low incidence category usage or when cost is an issue.

THE SURVEY QUESTIONNAIRE

The survey questionnaire should include a number of sections (described below), however it's best to keep online surveys short, ideally below 20 minutes. A recent study shows how bad respondent behaviors increase six-fold if we compare a 15-minute survey to a 30-minute survey (The Foundation of Quality ARF, 2009).[5] The shorter the survey—the better the completion rates.

If you have already conducted a usage and attitude (U&A) study for product/service category users this part can be excluded from the segmentation, otherwise a U&A section is necessary.

The following questionnaire sections will produce more actionable results:

- *Product category needs* can be broken down in different distinct elements if necessary, for example, in the case of a disease education video game it could be divided in console needs and actual game needs.

- *Demographics* includes gender, age, education, income, marital status, and so on.

- *Lifestyles and attitudes* includes entertainment, sports, attitude toward religion, politics, and attitudes toward health-related purchases in general.

- *Media consumption* includes both offline and online media including social media sites and other specific websites.

- *Behaviors* relates to the engagement with the product category, occasions of consumption, and so on (this section could be part of the U&A).

ANALYSIS OF RESULTS AND INTERPRETATION

According to Michael and Jaskolska (2004), segmentation is an art and a science.[6] It is a science because it uses sophisticated statistical techniques to create meaningful customer segments. It is an art because the attributes used in the segmentation questionnaire and the final segmentation option are based on the knowledge and experience of humans—that is, the agency researcher and the client's team.

There are many different ways to segment a market. However, here are some important considerations to make when segmenting:

1.   A healthcare customer takes "purchase" decisions based not only on objective factors but also on emotional ones.

2.   The emotional aspect can even affect the way "objective" factors are perceived (distortion of reality).

3.   The "purchase" decision process of a person might change with time based on life-stage.

4.   A factual database of prospective clients is not good enough for "state of the art" segmentation, because it does not explain the emotions that impact choices.

5.   Factual databases are often useful for targeting once the segments are specified, if they are able to provide distinct demographic characteristics for each segment. However these are poor substitutes for primary data that result from a segmentation survey when a company is interested to really focus on customer targets that make good business sense and best fits with its offer.

... segmentation is an art and a science.

The most popular of many segmentation methods available is cluster analysis combined with factor analysis. Before proceeding with this approach there are two questions to ask:

1.   Do we need to conduct factor analysis before we do clustering (segmentation) or should we just cluster (create segment options) based on all available factors/variables?

2.   If we do factor analysis before the cluster analysis do we group the factors/variables in a small number of consolidated factors, or do we just exclude the ones which are similar leaving the most distinctive ones to go on with the cluster analysis?

The more factors or variables we have, the more room there is for subjectivity. The result of cluster analysis is the creation of many segmentation options. Typically the options from three to six segments are considered.

This is when a large degree of "art" meets science in deciding which number of segments to accept.

There are two levels where artistic/creative interpretation need be applied:

1.   Selecting the statements or attributes or variables or factors (best practice is qualitative research with stakeholders before the segmentation survey).

2.   Deciding the number of segments based on the respondents' agreement with each factor.

To get the best out of the analysis and interpretation, both the research agency and the organization's management team have to engage and collaborate to come up with the decisions/answers together. They have to review multiple segment scenarios and once the number of segments is decided, based on homogeneity and plausibility, then they should be adequately "validated."

Differentiation and Positioning in Digital Communication

Kotler (2014)[7] defines differentiation as the process of adding meaningful and valued differences to distinguish the product from the competition. There are a number of differentiation dimensions and strategies for their accomplishment. Following are the main five dimensions according to Kotler:

- *Product differentiation.* The Internet differentiates itself by providing a limitless assortment of products (that is, product/service personalization; product packaging minimization to reduce waste and costs).

- *Service differentiation.* Customer service can be improved by 24-hour customer feedback through e-mail (that is, home delivery of groceries and medical products).

- *Channel differentiation.* The Internet is a location-free, time-free distribution and communication channel (that is, providing a highly specialized personal services and "do it yourself" website).

- *Image differentiation.* A company can differentiate itself by creating a unique experience online.

Positioning

Positioning involves developing a planned image among its competitors in the public's mind. The digital communicator's goals are to generate a position upon one or more bases which are useful and relevant to the consumer.

These are some of the main bases and strategies for positioning:

PRODUCT AND SERVICE ATTRIBUTE

May include features such as administration route, efficacy, access, and so on (that is, Tylenol does not sell online, but provides useful one-to-one features for pain relief and health information).

TECHNOLOGY POSITIONING

Indicates that an organization is innovative. As an example, Hawaii Medical Services Association, part of the Blue Cross & Blue Shield Association, is offering "virtual consults" to its members using technology developed by American Well. It enables an insured patient to contact any credentialed medical specialist on his or her insurer's network around the clock over the phone or by web (including webcam), video conference, secure messaging, or secure chat to help determine whether the medical issue can be worked out at home, requires an office visit, or warrants an urgent trip to an ER.

BENEFIT POSITIONING

Benefit positioning is usually a stronger foundation for positioning, because it answers the consumer question: What will this do for me? Pfizer, through its "morethanmedication" portal, offers online support groups.

USER CATEGORY

User category positioning relies on customer segments. Children's Healthcare of Atlanta offers 18' x 6' Interactive Videowalls for children which combines donor recognition, an educational play space, and a therapeutic place of comfort for children with severe physical and emotional needs and their families.

COMPETITOR POSITIONING

Organizations can position themselves versus a whole industry, a particular company, and relative industry position. Nevertheless, most of the organizations position themselves through benefits that offer advantages greater than their competitors.

Creating Competitive Advantage Online

Since your website—along with your Search Engine Marketing (SEM) and Internet Marketing—is part of your integrated Marketing, it is important to review your competition in order to excel.

To conclude this chapter we would like to give a quick look at online competitive analysis.

Thanks to "online competitive analysis" you will learn about which digital tools your competitors are using to inform or educate their audience and to promote their products and services. Most of all, if well conducted, an online competitive analysis will help you understand which strategies they are using and which tactics they are implementing. This will help you understand how your online presence, strategy, and tactics are positioned versus your direct and indirect competitors. Learning your competitors' strengths and weaknesses will help you develop a more focused and successful digital strategy, which will help you build a stronger competitive advantage.

Personalize the experience

Notes

1   Godin, S. (2011), *Linchpin: Are You Indispensable?* New York: Portfolio Trade.

2   Li, C. and Bernoff, J. (2008). Groundswell: Winning in a World Transformed by Social Technologies. *Harvard Business Press,* pp. 41–45.

3   Elliott, N. (2013), The Social Technographics Score helps marketers create better social strategies. Forrester Research, Inc. blogs [online] Available at http://blogs.forrester.com/nate_elliott/13–10–01-the_social_technographics_score_helps_marketers_create_better_social_strategies> [Accessed 15 December 2014].

4   Digital MR (2012), How To Use Needs Based Customer Segmentation. Integral reproduction with permission.

5   The Foundations of Quality ARF (2009), Knowledge Brief #2.

6   Michael, M.A. and Jaskolska, I. (2004), Is this Art or Science, *ESOMAR Book of Excellence.*

7   Kotler, P. and Armstrong, G. (2014), *Principles of Marketing,* 15th edition. Harlow: Pearson Education.

PART III

Designing and Implementing a Patient-Centered Digital Strategy

Chapter 6

Developing an Integrated Marketing Communications Strategy

LETIZIA AFFINITO

This chapter focuses further on how all communication must be planned and blended into carefully integrated programs to deliver a clear, consistent, and compelling message about its organization and its brands. We begin by examining the rapidly changing communications environment and the need for integrated marketing communications (IMC) and end by discussing the steps in developing marketing communications. In the next chapter we'll present the online marketing communications tools.

Let's start by looking at a good integrated communications approach.

Million Hearts: Help Us Prevent One Million Heart Attacks and Strokes by 2017—A Beautifully Integrated Healthcare Marketing Communications Campaign

Million Hearts© is a national initiative that has set an ambitious goal to prevent one million heart attacks and strokes by 2017. Launched by the Department of Health and Human Services (HHS) in September 2011, it aligns existing efforts, as well as creates new programs, to improve health across communities and help Americans live longer, more productive lives. The Centers for Disease Control and Prevention (CDC) and Centers for Medicare and Medicaid Services (CMS), co-leaders of Million Hearts© within HHS, are working alongside other federal agencies and private-sector organizations to make a long-lasting impact against cardiovascular disease. Key private-sector partners include the American Heart Association, and YMCA, among many others.

Million Hearts© aims to prevent heart disease and stroke by:

- improving access to effective care;

- improving the quality of care for the ABCS (**A**spirin for people at risk, **B**lood pressure control, **C**holesterol management and **S**moking cessation);

- focusing clinical attention on the prevention of heart attack and stroke;

- activating the public to lead a heart-healthy lifestyle;

- improving the prescription and adherence to appropriate medications for the ABCS;

It is a public–private initiative that involves multiple federal agencies and key private organizations. Collectively, these partnerships will help Million Hearts© leverage and further existing investments in cardiovascular disease prevention.

The CDC has acknowledged that social media can be more effective when integrated with traditional public health communication channels.

According to Heldman et al. (2013), although several communicators think social media can be used as independent, stand-alone channels different from "traditional" health communication tactics, several strategies, which work for social media, are the ones that work for and have been demonstrated to be effective for traditional health promotion or other mass communication efforts. Social media work best when integrated into a health communication strategy to support overarching communication goals and objectives.[1]

In fact, apart from being one of the best prevention campaigns in USA, Million Hearts© is also recognized for its wide-ranging marketing communications activities that encompass several "project lines" in the mix as communicated through various media. There are a number of reasons why CDC's marketing communications strategy works so well. One of these is that the organization embraces IMC by carefully integrating and coordinating its communication channels to deliver a clear, consistent, comprehensive, and compelling message about heart disease prevention and various ways to pursue it. This is clearly evident in HHS's use of advertising, public relations, direct marketing, and other marketing communications tools. Meanwhile, a key factor in its marketing communications that cannot be ignored is its strapline "Be One in a Million Hearts," which was introduced to encourage people empowerment. The introduction of this strapline became necessary as HHS acknowledged that people are bombarded with many health communications messages from different sources, and a clear-cut message on how the organization is positioned to help people solve their problems was fundamentally needed. For example, as detailed on the company's website, the slogan communicates that preventing one million heart attacks and strokes by 2017 requires work and a commitment to change from all, and that it was important to instill the idea of a "shared goal" among people and institutions.

The consistency with which this message spreads across all of the marketing communications media that HHS uses is noteworthy. Evidence shows that the organization uses the traditional marketing tools effectively, and it has been spending more than the sector average on every one of the media it uses since 2011.

By now it is clear that the elements of the marketing environment keep changing, and so are customers' modes of communication. This is emphasized by the fact that we are now in the digital age; hence it is logical that the relevant tools associated with these developments be integrated with the traditional media toward making a compelling case about the brand of the organization. This is exactly what HHS does. The Million Hearts© campaign has a presence in various social media, including Facebook, Twitter, and YouTube, which are managed by a dedicated team of experts through which it offers a personalized service to the big fan base in the USA.

Despite the increase in the number of means of communications available to HHS, its focus on the key messages still remains "Be One in a Million Hearts." It basically ensures that its mass-media advertisements effectively deliver the same message as shown in the PR and advertising promotion stimuli, which is consistent with what is shown on its website and also corroborates what is communicated through the company's various social media links.

The marketing information about the Million Hearts© Initiative and its tools, as shown on social media, are coherently integrated with other traditional media to echo the message.

Simply put, the marketing information about the Million Hearts© Initiative and its resources/tools as shown on YouTube, Facebook, Twitter, and other social media are coherently integrated with other traditional media to echo the message.

As expected in an effective marketing communications process, HHS often begins by identifying its target audience. This helps the organization to decide on the content of its message, as well as how it will be delivered, when will it be delivered, who will deliver it, and where it will be delivered. It also determines the communication objectives early enough in the process for successful outcomes. HHS emphasizes that people pass through the people-readiness stages—awareness, knowledge, liking, preference, conviction, and "purchase." Accordingly it sets its marketing communications objectives to be consistent with this model as circumstances demand. It carefully designs the message in such a way that ensures consistency between all the marketing communication tools used, selects the message source, collects feedback, and selects the marketing communication budget in relation to the appropriate mix of the marketing tools. As an example, in a move to strengthen its IMC system, in March, 2012 CDC launched the first-ever paid national tobacco education campaign—Tips From Former Smokers (Tips). The Tips campaign, which profiles real people—not actors—who are living with serious long-term health effects from smoking and second-hand smoke exposure, has continued through 2013 and 2014.

The marketing information about the Million Hearts© Initiative and its tools, as shown on social media, are coherently integrated with other traditional media to echo the message.

Tips ads focus on health issues caused by smoking or exposure to secondhand smoke.

The Tips campaign engages doctors, nurses, dentists, pharmacists, and many other healthcare providers so they can encourage their smoking patients to quit for good.

Partners from across the public and private health sectors, including federal agencies; doctors, nurses, pharmacists, and other HCPs; private insurers; businesses; health advocacy groups; and community organizations, will support Million Hearts© through a wide range of activities.

Examples of Million Hearts[©] activities include:

- Educational campaigns to increase awareness about heart disease prevention and empower patients to take control of their heart health.

- Use of health information technology and quality improvement initiatives to standardize and improve the delivery of care for high blood pressure and high cholesterol.

- Community efforts to promote smoke-free air policies and reduce sodium in the food supply.

Overall some key metrics of the Million Hearts[©] Initiative include:

- more than one million visits to the Million Hearts[©] website;

- E-newsletter distribution to more than 48,000 subscribers.

- more than 140 free downloadable resources, from infographics to heart attack survivor testimonial videos to provider tools;

- more than 63,000 Facebook fans and 15,000 Twitter followers as of August, 2014.

Going forward, Million Hearts[©] will be successful through the long-term implementation, ongoing coordination of efforts, and ability to achieve sustained community and clinical innovations.[2]

Key success factors can be summarized as follows:

COLLABORATION

Since 2012, Million Hearts[©] has garnered the support of many organizations, including more than 100 partners that have formally committed to specific activities, such as the Association of State and Territorial Health Officials (ASTHO), National Committee for Quality Assurance (NCQA), Association of Black Cardiologists, Kaiser Permanente, Men's Health Network, Preventive Cardiovascular Nurses Association, American Heart Association, National Forum for Heart Disease and Stroke Prevention, and many others. The most exciting and promising collaborations in Million Hearts© bring together the complementary assets of the public health and healthcare sectors.

OPTIMIZING CARE

Million Hearts© asks HCPs to prioritize the ABCS because high performance on these measures leads to fewer disabling and deadly cardiovascular events. Since 2012, many HCPs have accepted the challenge and adopted health tools and technologies and innovative care delivery models to support their ABCS goals.

FOCUS ON CHANGING THE ENVIRONMENT

While working hard to improve clinical care, the Million Hearts© Initiative focuses also on improving the environments in which people live, learn, work, and play to make healthy living easier. Million Hearts© inspires communities to take their own action to address the cardiovascular risks associated with smoking, high sodium consumption, and trans fat intake.

As we move into the twenty-first century, healthcare communication managers face some new marketing communication realities.

Two major factors are changing the face of today's marketing communications.

First, as mass markets have fragmented and patient-centricity has become an imperative, healthcare communication managers are shifting away from mass marketing communications and developing focused marketing communication programs, designed to build closer relationships with patients and generate increased value in more narrowly defined micro-markets.

Second, enormous improvements in information technology are speeding up the change toward segmented marketing: new technologies provide new communications opportunities to reach smaller customer segments with more tailored messages.

Market fragmentation has resulted in media fragmentation into more focused media that better match today's targeting strategies. Today, marketers have more choices than ever regarding how and where to promote or advertise products and services. In addition to traditional methods, such as print advertising and direct marketing, you have e-mail marketing, web-based

> ## ... enormous improvements in information technology are speeding up the change toward segmented marketing ...

advertising and multiple social media sites, such as Facebook, Twitter, and YouTube, as well as mobile marketing.

Given this new communications environment, health communication managers must rethink the roles of various media and promotion mix tools.

Marketers are using a greater variety of focused communication tools in an attempt to reach their distinct target markets.

Integrating social media engagement with offline experiences enables involvement in both the virtual and real world, and offers dedicated social media users the chance to obtain exclusive access to events and opportunities. Examples of online/offline engagement include NASA Social,[3] which provides in-person opportunities for users who currently engage on NASA social media accounts, such as meet and greet sessions and behind the scenes events to connect with NASA scientists. The American Red Cross also offers training to individuals on using social media on behalf of the Red Cross. During disasters, these Digital Disaster Volunteers report back to the Red Cross social media team and "monitor, engage, and report on activity surrounding specific disasters."

Why Integrated Marketing Communication is Important

The change from mass marketing to targeted marketing exposes patients to a greater variety of marketing communication initiatives from and about the organization from a range of sources. Consequently, customers, often, don't distinguish between message sources the way communicators do. In the patient's mind, advertising messages from different media, such as television, magazines, or online sources, confuse into one. Messages delivered through diverse promotional tactics, such as advertising, personal selling, sales promotion, public relations, or direct marketing, become part of a single message about the organization. Differing messages from these diverse sources can generate confused organization images and brand positioning. In addition, while the benefits of online healthcare marketing are clear, they shouldn't be the sole means for communication with a customer base. The population in the most need of healthcare is older people, a demographic

In the patient's mind, advertising messages from different media, such as television, magazines, or online sources, confuse into one.

not exactly known for its familiarity with technological tools. HCPs should embrace digital marketing wholeheartedly while still maintaining current forms of offline marketing, so long as those marketing methods have proven themselves to be successful.

Frequently, organizations don't succeed in integrating their different communication channels. The result is a mixture of communications to patients.

To get over this potential risk today many companies are using IMC by strategically integrating and coordinating their many communications channels to deliver a clear, consistent, and compelling message about the organization and its products (Figure 6.1).[4]

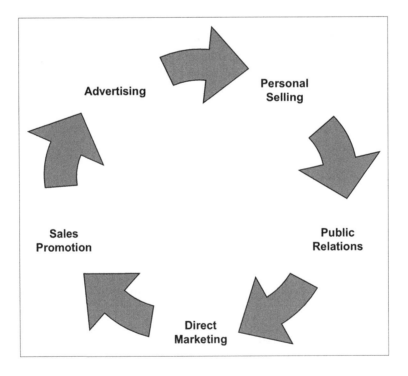

Figure 6.1   Integrated marketing communications

Source: Adapted from Kotler, P. and Armstrong, G. (2014), *Principles of Marketing*, 15th edition. Harlow: Pearson Education, p. 431.

IMC develops a solid brand identity in the marketplace by binding together and strengthening all images and messages. Through IMC all corporate messages, positioning and images, and identity are coordinated across all (marketing communications) settings. As a result, the PR materials contents are consistent with the direct mail campaign, and the advertising and the website recall the identical "look and feel."

Developing an effective IMC plan requires the identification of all contact points at which the patient may encounter the organization, its products, and its brands. Each brand contact will convey a message. The organization must struggle to convey a consistent and positive message at all contact points.

Frequently, organizations don't succeed in integrating their different communication channels. The result is a mixture of communications to patients.

IMC results in an overall marketing communication strategy designed to demonstrate how the organization and its products can support patients in solving their problems.

An IMC will allow you not only to double your reach, but also to tap competitors and show patients that you're a leader in the industry.

Developing a Successful Integrated Marketing Campaign

As mentioned earlier, IMC involves recognizing the target audience and designing a well-coordinated communication program to generate the expected audience reaction (Kotler and Armstrong, 2014).[5] Communication programs must be developed for specific segments, niches, and even individuals, because customers differ. In addition, nowadays, with the increasing use of the new interactive communications technologies, companies must ask not only, "How can we reach our customers?" but also, "How can we find ways to let our customers reach us?"

As a consequence, the communications process should start with an accurate assessment of all the potential interactions/touch points which target healthcare customers may have with the product/service and the company (patient experience).

Even though there is not a standard procedure to developing an effective IMC, the following are some of the main steps that you should take to achieve your goals and create value for your audiences.[6]

- Identifying the target audience

  Your audience may be potential or current patients, those who make the buying decision (that is, the patient or caregiver) or those who influence it (that is, physicians, insurance companies, and other payers). The audience may be individuals, institutions, patients associations, professional organizations, groups, special publics, or the general public. Based on the characteristics of the target audience, you must decide on *what* will be said, *how* it will be said, *when* it will be said, *where* it will be said, and *who* will say it. Of course, those decisions are dictated by the needs of the audience.

  It's crucial to clearly identify who your target audience is through socialgraphics (see Chapter 5), to develop effective key messages and to identify the best communication channels to connect with them.

... companies must ask not only, "How can we reach our customers?" but also, "How can we find ways to let our customers reach us?"

- Determining the desired response

  In most cases, the final response in healthcare communications is behavior change. But behavior change is the result of a long process of consumer decision-making. The target audience may be in any of six "buyer" readiness stages, the stages that consumers typically pass through on their way to making a purchase (Kotler and Armstrong, 2014) (Figure 6.2).[7]

These stages are *awareness, knowledge, liking, preference, conviction,* and *purchase.* The marketing communicator needs to learn where the target audience stands and to what stage it needs to be led.

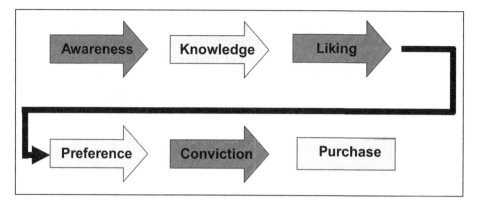

Figure 6.2   Buyer readiness stages

Source: Adapted from Kotler, P. and Armstrong, G. (2014), *Principles of Marketing*, 15th edition. Harlow: Pearson Education, p. 436.

The marketing communicator's target market may be totally unaware of the product/service/disease/project, know only its name, or know little about it. The communicator must first build *awareness* and *knowledge*.

Developing an Impactful Message

The message should generate *attention*, grasp *interest*, stimulate *desire*, and get *action* (a framework known as the AIDA model).[8] Nevertheless, in reality, few messages get the consumer all the way from awareness to purchase, but the AIDA framework suggests the qualities of a good message.

In putting together the message, you must solve three problems: (1) what to say (*message content*), (2) how to say it logically (*message structure*), and (3) how to say it symbolically (*message format*).

CONTENT

The communicator must find an appeal or theme that will generate the expected response. There are three types of appeals: rational, emotional, and moral.

- *Rational appeals* refers to the audience's self-interest. They show that the product will generate the desired benefits (that is, product's efficacy, safety, quality, economy, value, or performance).

- *Emotional appeals* try to inspire either negative or positive emotions which can motivate purchase (that is, positive emotional appeals such as love, pride, joy, and humor). Communicators can also use negative emotional appeals such as fear, guilt, and shame, which get people to do things they should (that is, take their medicine, brush their teeth, monitor blood pressure), or to stop doing things they shouldn't (that is, smoke, drink too much, eat fatty foods).

- *Moral appeals* are aimed at the audience's sense of what is "right" and "proper" to urge people to support such social causes as an aid to the needy, or combat such social problems as prevention, breast cancer.

In the healthcare industry, moral and rational appeals are mostly used. The true emotional values are, in fact, rarely communicated. The majority of the campaigns tend to widely deliver the same facts and product/service functional features. Nevertheless, examples of campaigns also delivering an emotional appeal, built on the patients' true needs and concerns, demonstrates that it helps to better relate with the audience and make a difference. Starting with a research can be very helpful in finding a clue from which start building your entire IMC (that is, the Real Beauty Campaign for Dove; morethanmedication digital campaign from Pfizer).

STRUCTURE

When structuring your marketing message, you must decide whether to offer a conclusion or leave it to the audience. Recent research, considering the impact of social media, shows that asking questions and giving buyers the opportunity to reach their own opinions can generate enhanced outcomes. Another structure topic relates to the decision to communicate a one-sided claim—highlighting exclusively the product's strengths—or a two-sided claim—boldly promoting the product's strengths while also wisely presenting its weaknesses. Healthcare marketing almost always requires a "two-sided" approach for ethical and legal reasons. When pharmaceutical companies promote prescription drugs to consumers and physicians in the US, the Federal Food, Drug, and Cosmetic Act (FD&C Act) requires that major side effects and important safety information must be mentioned along with the benefits.

FORMAT

In an online ad, or in an online newsletter, the digital health communicator has to decide on the headline, copy, illustration, and color. The Internet is mainly a visual medium and colors may be the simplest and most effective way to get your message to your online visitors. Understanding color psychology and the unconscious and imperceptible effect of color on the visitor's emotions, can help you make your best choice of colors in designing a website capable of capturing the interest of your visitor, and potential customer.

Starting with a research can be very helpful in finding a clue from which start building your entire IMC

To attract attention, advertisers often use novelty and contrast; eye-catching pictures and headlines; distinctive formats; message size and position; and color, shape, and movement. If the message will be carried over a webinar, the communicator must choose words, sounds, and voices.

If the message is to be carried on a video, then all these elements plus body language have to be planned. Presenters plan their facial expressions, gestures, dress, posture, and hairstyle. In addition to the role which color can play in communicating information, color can also affect attitude, well-being, and motivation in healthcare.

Mapping and Selecting Media

Before focusing on digital communication we will take a quick look at the main media channels used in IMC in this section.

Personal communication channels. Two or more persons communicate straightforwardly with each other face to face, over the telephone, or even through the mail or e-mail. Personal communication channels work well because they provide for personal addressing and feedback. Organizations control some personal communication channels, such as salespeople, directly from the company. Nevertheless, some personal communications about product/service and/or related initiatives can get to the healthcare customers through other channels, such as opinion leaders, patient advocates, healthcare providers guides, and others, sharing their opinions with target healthcare customers, not directly controlled by the organization.

It can, sometimes, even be neighbors, friends, family members, carers, and associates talking to target healthcare consumers ("word-of-mouth influence").

... the message's impact on the target audience is highly influenced by how the communicator is perceived by the audience.

Personal influence carries great weight for products that are lifesaving, highly innovative, expensive, risky, or highly visible. In order to put personal communication channels to work for them, healthcare organizations can create "opinion leaders" by involving certain authoritative medical professionals and/or researchers in clinical studies, scientific/educational boards, or giving them exclusive access to use a medical product for their patients (see Chapter 4).

Non-personal communication channels. Media that deliver messages without personal contact or feedback such as major media (that is, print media broadcast media, display media), atmospheres (that is, designed environments that create or reinforce the buyer's leanings toward buying a product, for example physicians' offices and hospitals are designed to communicate confidence and other qualities that might be valued by their clients), and events (that is, press conferences, road shows, grand openings, exhibits, and other events arranged by public relations departments).

When picking your channels, in addition to asking, "Which channels do my healthcare customers use?" ask yourself, "What are the channels' strengths and weaknesses?" "How will they help me reach my communication objectives?" You can get better results by focusing on the most effective channels than trying to be all encompassing.

The Increasing Importance of the Message Source

In Chapter 4 we discussed how, in either personal or non-personal communication, the message's impact on the target audience is highly influenced by how the communicator is perceived by the audience. Messages presented by credible sources are more convincing. Therefore, many healthcare organizations employ opinion leaders and celebrities to deliver their key messages.

Leverage creativity

Notes

1   Heldman, A.B., Schindelar, J. and Weaver, J.B. III (2013), Social Media Engagement and Public Health Communication: Implications for Public Health Organizations Being Truly "Social". *Public Health Reviews*, p. 35: epub ahead of print.

2   Centers for Disease Control and Prevention USA (2014), Preventing 1 Million Heart Attacks and Strokes—A Turning Point for Impact [online]. Available at http://www.cdc.gov/cdcgrandrounds/archives/2014/september2014.htm [Accessed 02 December 2014].

3   National Aeronautics and Space Administration. Connect and collaborate with NASA (2014) [online]. Available at http://www.nasa.gov/connect/social/index.html [Accessed 02 December 2014].

4   Kotler, P. and Armstrong, G. (2014), *Principles of Marketing*, 15th edition. Harlow: Pearson Education, p. 436.

5   Kotler, P. and Armstrong, G. (2014), *Principles of Marketing*, 15th edition. Harlow: Pearson Education, pp. 429–440.

6   CXO Media (2014), 7 Ways to Create a Successful Integrated Marketing Campaign [online]. Available at www.cio.com [Accessed 25 November 2014].

7   Kotler, P. and Armstrong, G. (2014), *Principles of Marketing*, 15th edition. Harlow: Pearson Education, p. 436.

8   Kotler, P. and Armstrong, G. (2014), *Principles of Marketing*, 15th edition. Harlow: Pearson Education, p. 436.

Chapter 7

Integrating Digital into Your Marketing Communication Mix

LETIZIA AFFINITO AND JOHN MACK

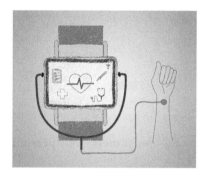

A digital communication strategy offers brands and healthcare organizations new and unique ways of engaging with their customers and audiences to a greater degree than has been previously possible, although many long-standing marketing and communication principles still apply. Some marketing experts have even likened the Internet to "direct marketing on steroids."

Today, however, social media allows healthcare marketers to transcend the traditional direct marketing approach by engaging consumers and patients in a dialogue and tapping into UGC. Without any doubt, the greatest opportunity—and challenge—for digital health communication in the twenty-first century is implementing an integrated Web 2.0 enabled campaign. Using new digital social media technologies, healthcare communicators can push their messages out and interact with appropriate audience in ways that were not possible just a few years ago before the advent of social media.

Consumers and physicians are spending more and more time accessing digital media via desktop and mobile devices and less and less time reading newspapers and magazines, listening to the radio, or watching broadcast TV. Media spending by all advertisers—not just healthcare marketers—needs to shift to the new channels that their audiences are using. This shift is overdue, especially for the pharmaceutical industry (see Figure 7.1).

If a digital communication campaign is well-conceived, it can surely lead to better health outcomes for patients and higher profits for healthcare organizations: a win–win.

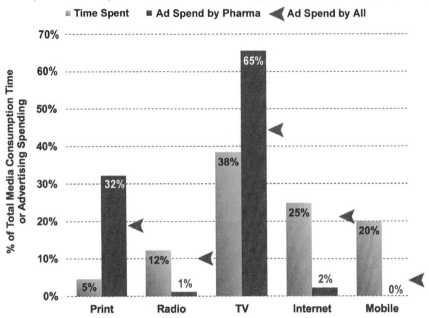

Figure 7.1   Percent time spent in media by consumers vs. percent advertising spending by pharma

Source: Pharma Marketing Blog; http://pharmamkting.blogspot.com/2014/05/pharma-dtc-advertising-spend-vs-time.html [accessed 21 December 2014].

Note: Arrows indicate level of spending for all industries as reported by Mary Meeker, partner at Kleiner Perkins Caufield Byers. Pharma spending data comes from Nielsen.

New Digital Direct-Marketing Technologies

To begin with, what do we mean by "direct marketing?"

Direct marketing is a channel-agnostic form of advertising by which a healthcare organization can communicate directly with the customer, whether they are consumers, patients, or HCPs. Since we are concerned with digital media, we'll focus on the following channels:

- interactive websites;

- e-mail;

- mobile apps and cell phone text messaging;

- online display ads;

- social media, including YouTube, Twitter, Facebook, and so on.

These channels are often "integrated" with offline channels that may include mass media (newspaper, magazine, TV and radio) ads, promotional letters/mailers, and specialized channels such as outdoor billboards, and even movie theatre ads. An integrated marketing strategy is a great way to capture the attention of consumers and patients and build your business for the future. Key to the strategy is to understand the media preferences of your audience.

A SUCCESSFUL, INTEGRATED MOBILE APP AD CAMPAIGN

According to the 2014 US Mobile App Report by Comscore, total US digital media time spent has jumped 24 percent in the past year, driven by a surge in mobile app usage, which increased 52 percent. Despite this, mobile apps have not been attracting the dollars its audience warrants, says Comscore.

One pharma company, however, has cleverly and successfully promoted one of its drugs via a mobile app.

That company is Astellas, which partnered with RunPee, a movie-viewing mobile app that tells users the best time to "run and pee" without missing the best scenes, to deliver highly effective ads for Myrbetriq, a treatment for over-active bladder (OAB).

The campaign integrated in-cinema advertising that promoted the mobile app, the app itself—which appealed to an appropriate audience at an appropriate time—and an interstitial mobile ad that drove viewers to a mobile-optimized product information website.

Astellas ran 60-second Myrbetriq direct-to-consumer (DTC) advertisements in movie theaters nationwide in the US in the summer of 2014. At the end of the DTC ad, which ran before the movie started, was a 10-second tag that encouraged moviegoers to download the RunPee app, which was free because Astellas paid the $0.99 download price during the campaign. This tactic was successful in getting consumers aware of the app, which was downloaded about 80,000 times during the campaign, which exceeded the goal set by Astellas by 50 percent.

Each time the app was run, another Myrbetriq DTC ad was served before the app would open. This contextually relevant mobile ad included the Myrbetriq bladder character sitting in a director's chair who directed viewers to the website to learn more about the product.

Astellas saw very strong clickthrough rates to the website—about 12 percent of people who downloaded the app clicked through to the website. Typically, clickthrough rates for interstitial pharma mobile ads like this are more like 0.6 percent.

The integrated Myrbetriq campaign is a good example of how healthcare marketers can use digital and mobile technology to reach a targeted group of consumers with timely information that is relevant to them and that motivates them to take action. It also confirms how important mobile is becoming in the promotional mix.

Although mobile apps are sexy, you should be aware that two-thirds of smartphone users do NOT download apps. From that perspective, it's clear that healthcare marketers should probably not waste their time (and money) developing mobile apps and then expect a broad base of smartphone users to download them—not unless they have an approach similar to Astella's, which incentivized a targeted and receptive audience to download the app and not unless the app meets an unmet need. It's also helpful if the app is free or sponsored so the consumer does not have to pay for it.

Keep in mind that non-digital channels are still important components of the healthcare communication mix for specific audiences. The Myrbetriq RunPee campaign, for example, is just part of a broader effort by Astellas to team up with patient groups such as Red Hot Mamas to raise awareness of women's health issues, including menopause and overactive bladder. Astellas also ran typical DTC ads in magazines and on TV that featured the same Myrbetriq character that appeared in the mobile ad embedded in the RunPee app.

Marketing Mix

There are many options that marketers consider when determining the appropriate mix of channels for any given communication program. It is convenient to consider several lists of channels: one for reaching physicians, one for reaching consumers and patients, and one for reaching both. There is much overlap—several channels may be used for both physicians and consumers.

General promotional mix ingredients (used to reach both physicians and consumers):

- product websites

- third-party website sponsorship

- call center

- direct mail

- e-mail

- mobile technology (apps, SMS, and so on)

- podcasts

- search engines

- national TV

- social media

- spot TV

- telemarketing

- web banner ads.

Physician-specific promotional mix ingredients:

- eDetailing

- point of care marketing (ePrescribing)

- sales representative

- journal ads (print)

- scientific meetings/exhibits.

Consumer-specific promotional mix ingredients:

- consumer-generated content (buzz and blogs)

- health fairs

- outdoor and event venues (billboards, sports)

- pharmacy programs

- magazines and newspapers (print)

- physician office programs.

FACTORS THAT DETERMINE THE MIX

For any given communication campaign, healthcare marketers may use the following factors to set the budget and allocate funds to specific channels:

- reach and frequency criteria—reach defines the audience of each channel;

- past experience;

- matching competitive budgets;

- recommendation of the agency or outside consultants;

- formal analysis of ROI or profit goals;

- gut/other.

These days, "reach and frequency" cannot be the only goal of healthcare marketing.

Obviously, reach and frequency are staples of any promotional campaign. Reach is the total number of people who are exposed to a given medium such as TV. A large number of households in the US and Europe have TVs. So TV offers incredible reach. Almost as many people also have Internet access and therefore digital media also offers incredible reach. Reach alone, however, does not guarantee how many people will see the message. If the message is repeated—that is, broadcast more frequently—it is more likely to be seen.

These days, "reach and frequency" cannot be the only goal of healthcare marketing. Perhaps your reach and frequency are fine, but you also need to improve targeting to reach the intended audience and engage them once your reach them. New media channels offer the best opportunity for targeting and engaging consumers and HCPs.

Where consumers go online first, however, is not the full story. It's where they end up that's most important.

Websites are the Core of Your Strategy

According to Pew Internet, nearly three-quarters of American Internet users have sought out health information online during the past year (2012). 77 percent of online health seekers say they began their last session at a search engine (Google, Bing, or Yahoo). Another 13 percent say they began at a site that specializes in health information, like WebMD. Just 2 percent say they started their research at a more general site like Wikipedia and an additional 1 percent say they started at a social network site like Facebook.[1]

Where consumers go online first, however, is not the full story. It's where they end up that's most important. Obviously, search engines are critical in determining what websites consumers ultimately visit. Consequently, when you build a website, it must be (1) search-engine friendly—this is done by a process called "search-engine optimization" (SEO); and (2) advertised in search engines so that it appears at the top of the list.

A well-designed website is the most important component of an online communication strategy. Gone are the days, however, when a website is merely "brochureware;" that is, just an online version of a printed product or service brochure. That was the hallmark of Web 1.0 technology.

Today, websites are more dynamic and can include many social media features such as Facebook like and Twitter buttons that allow visitors to share the content with their social media friends and followers. Many websites also include embedded YouTube videos that may be used to tell patient stories or inform visitors about products and services.

Your website must also be platform-agnostic, which means it must be especially easy to view and navigate on mobile devices such as smartphones and tablets as well as "Phablets."

Such websites may be costly to create and maintain, especially if the information must be updated frequently. According to recent research by benchmarking firm, Best Practices, LLC, more than half of the participating companies averaged more than $100,000 in annual spending on website development and maintenance.[2] Of course, the cost depends on many factors and it is possible to maintain a compelling website for much less than $100,000 per year.

The regulated pharmaceutical industry probably spends millions of dollars per website, especially drug.com sites, which are among the first sites that patients visit when their doctors prescribe a specific treatment. Of course, branded drug websites are only intended for audiences in the US and New Zealand where DTC advertising of prescription (Rx) drugs is legal. But pharma companies also launch and maintain hundreds of unbranded "disease-awareness" websites that can be accessed by any one, anywhere. Disease-awareness sites are better suited to capture patient visitors at a specific stage of the patient journey: when they are first diagnosed. After all, patients are not likely to visit a drug website before they even know what their problem is.

A well-designed website is the most important component of an online communication strategy.

Pharmaceutical disease-awareness sites often link to "treatment options," which can include links to specific branded drug sites—most likely the drug manufactured by the company that is hosting the disease information site. Other healthcare organizations such as hospitals may also host disease information websites or micro-sites that also link to their treatment facilities, attending specialists, and so on.

Social media is especially useful for disease-awareness campaign. Unity Stoakes, President, OrganizedWisdom, a health-focused, social networking site for consumers and physicians, suggests some good reasons why healthcare organizations should engage in social media. "The more they participate and the more they introduce their messages, education and content into the conversation," says Stoakes, "the more likely these messages will be heard, repurposed, regurgitated, verified in the same way that much of the content on Wikipedia is checked and sourced."[3]

GlaxoSmithkline (GSK) was the first pharmaceutical company to sponsor a disease-awareness YouTube video. The video, titled "My Dad has Restless Leg Syndrome," was been viewed more than 73,000 times within a period of several months after it was uploaded in October, 2006. It shows a toppling dominoes cascade that starts with the dad kicking in bed and ending with the "money shot," which includes some information about restless legs syndrome (that is, "a million people in the UK suffer from RLS") and a URL where the viewer can go to find more information about RLS. The website recommends that visitors talk to their doctor about treatment. That's about as close as you can get to providing treatment information online to consumers in the UK. In the US, on the other hand, unbranded sites can link out to the product site. These days, pharmaceutical websites embed YouTube videos directly into the site, very often on the home page.

The Importance of Search and Video

We'll get back to websites and discuss how to engage site visitors later in this chapter. Right now, however, is a good time to discuss how to drive visitors to your website. One of the most effective ways to drive traffic to websites is via search engines such as Google and YouTube, which are the #1 and #2 search engines, respectively, by volume.

A 2015 national (US) consumer "Pulse of Online Health" Survey fielded by Makovsky Health and Kelton in January, 2015[4] determined that 80 percent of Americans were willing to visit a pharma-sponsored Web site (e.g., a drug.com site), which is a high percentage but somewhat less than the 88% who were willing to do so in 2010. Of the 80 percent of Americans willing to visit a pharma-sponsored website, those 66 and older were more likely to visit the site if a healthcare professional recommended it (52 percent). Doctor recommendation matters less to Millennials, with 41 percent visiting a site based on physician suggestion. On the other hand, Millennials are 23 percent more likely to be motivated by an advertisement to visit a pharma-sponsored website than those 66 and older.

Disease-awareness sites are better suited to capture patient visitors at a specific stage of the patient journey: when they are first diagnosed.

With regard to social media, almost two-thirds (66 perecnt) of Americans would use a mobile app to manage health-related issues. Millennials are leading the digital health charge, as they are more than twice as likely to express interest in using a mobile app to manage their health compared to their parents (Baby Boomers aged 66 and older).

Online search is a critical method by which consumers find health information on the Internet after perhaps getting recommendations from friends or physicians and seeing ads on TV. Makovsky data, for example, show US consumers spend an average of 135 hours looking for health information on the Internet annually. PEW Internet surveys suggest that worldwide, about 4.5 percent of all Internet searches are for health-related information and 52 million American adults—55 percent percent of Internet users—are Internet "health seekers;" that is, access health or medical information on the Internet at least once per month. These factoids are not lost on pharmaceutical marketers who devote an estimated 40 percent of their online marketing budgets to advertising on search engines; for example, buying keywords so that their websites come up first in search results on those words.

The future of SEM is to develop and integrate digital assets such as video and maybe even blogs and other social media into the marketing mix.

SEM is evolving rapidly and it's no longer simply a matter of purchasing keywords on Google. These days you need to differentiate yourself through linking and social media, including YouTube, in order to get top ranking in search engines. Perhaps two out of the top ten search results are social networking sites. According to experts, organic search is evolving to integrate more social networking (that is, consumer-generated content), video, and enhanced media into the results.

The future of SEM is to develop and integrate digital assets such as video and maybe even blogs and other social media into the marketing mix. Johnson & Johnson, for example, is doing that with its innovative YouTube channel. It makes sense to develop these other web assets that come up as the result of "organic search." That gives consumers and HCPs looking for health-related videos and blogs the opportunity to see your message in other areas of the web than just your product, corporate, or disease awareness website.

As opposed to buying banner ads and other types of online advertising, SEM allows advertisers to pay for ads that "perform" in terms of delivering traffic. With paid search, often called "keyword buys" or "pay per click," advertisers only pay for prospects who are actually interested in learning more about a product or service. These payments are sometimes determined by a blind auction model, where marketers can enter a maximum price that they are willing to pay for placement of their keyword ad.

Mitch Bernstein, currently SVP New Business Development at Havas Media, offered the following SEM tips in a *Pharma Marketing News* article:[5]

TIP 1. Optimize your website for Natural Search. Optimizing your web assets (SEM or SEO) requires more than simply "tweaking" your site. It takes an ongoing effort to make sure that the site content is optimized for search engine algorithms, which are constantly updated to prevent "gaming" the system.

While paid search has generated a lot of the buzz in marketing circles, natural search results are actually responsible for as much as 80–85 percent of search-related traffic. Natural results are not labeled as "Paid," "Featured," or "Sponsored" and are not for sale. Competition for first-page visibility is fierce, and is determined by a combination of content, brand relevance, and a whole host of technical factors that include linking strategies, coding style, and keyword density. Natural search results are generated by complex and constantly evolving algorithms, or "spiders," unique to individual search engines, and the results can change frequently. To stay ahead, companies must develop sophisticated content strategies to win the war of visibility.

Prominent visibility is best attained by continually addressing the dynamic nature of the leading search engines, the content of the site being optimized, and the content on sites hosted by competitors. Now, content alone is not enough. Starting in April, 2015, Google gives mobile-friendly sites a higher ranking in searches made by phones and tablets. This is important because Internet access via mobile devices surpasses that of desktop computers (for more on mobile optimization, see page 158).

SEARCH GLOSSARY

Algorithm—In the context of search engines, it is the mathematical programming system used to determine which web pages are displayed in search results.

Cost-per-click (CPC)—The CPC is the amount you pay each time a user clicks on your ad.

Keyword—Keywords are the words users type in to define a search. The keywords you choose for a given ad are used to target users searching on those keywords and thus deliver your ads to potential customers.

Link Popularity—A count of the number of links pointing (inbound links) at a website. Many search engines now count linkage in their algorithms.

Natural Search Optimization (NSO)—The process of matching code to Search Engine algorithms, so that website content can be fully spidered and indexed by the leading search engines.

Organic Search Results—listings on search engine results pages that appear because of their relevance to the search terms, as opposed to their being advertisements.

PageRank—The search engine Google is based upon link counting. The more quality links that a website has, the better its "page rank" (PR). PageRank values can range from 0 to 10.

Search Engine Spam—The submission of pages that are intended to rank artificially high by various unethical techniques. These can include submitting hundreds of slightly different pages designed to rank high, small invisible text, or word scrambled pages.

Spider—The main program used by search engines to retrieve web pages to include in their database.

TIP 2. Buy keywords. While almost anybody can buy paid media keywords, you'll want to make sure that ad copy is crafted to your audience, that you're managing bids on the different engines, and that response tracking systems are in place to measure the impact.

A good search marketing campaign will feature keyword lists built with proper derivatives, and website copy that is drafted directly to that cohort. When a particular keyword or string performs well, marketers can then leverage the intelligence behind that data to drive brand awareness and sales in the short term, making your program more successful.

TIP 3. Hire an experienced SEM provider. For many people, the simplest option is to hire an expert. When seeking an SEM provider, be sure that they blend multiple strategies to drive results. paid search encompasses both CPC keyword advertising as well as paid inclusion. CPC keyword ads are set apart from the "natural" results from a search and are labeled as such by their placement. Paid Inclusion results are listings that look like natural or algorithmic results, but are actually paid for by marketers. Instead of pricing that works on an auction system, paid inclusion results are generally set at a fixed price per click, depending on the type of term being bought.

What's Your Video SEM Strategy?

Video syndication via Youtube—that is, placing your video on YouTube—is much more effective than putting it directly on your website without using Youtube. Why? Simply because more people will find it and view it on Youtube, which reaches more 18–34-year-old US adults than any cable network. In addition, YouTube processes more than three billion searches per month.[6]

According to Makovsky, 11 percent of US adults have accessed YouTube specifically for health information in 2015.

Aside from Youtube's importance as a search engine in driving visitors to your website, there are several other reasons why YouTube is an important part of any online healthcare communication strategy (source of data: Google Internal statistics; October, 2013)[7]:

1.   YouTube has over one billion monthly users worldwide; it's the third most viewed website (with one billion daily views on mobile devices, which are often used by healthcare consumers at the point of care);

2.   42–65 percent of patients click on YouTube-sponsored listings;

3.   YouTube videos are included in Google results—in fact, since Google now owns YouTube, you can expect that Youtube videos get preferential treatment in Google searches;

4.   video is the best way to increase engagement with patients and humanize your business. As mentioned in a previous chapter, many healthcare organizations, including drug companies, create patient testimonial videos to help convey their marketing messages;

5.   until health literacy increases dramatically, video is much more effective than print in communicating healthcare information;

6.   healthcare organizations often create video for other purposes and can easily "repurpose" these videos on Youtube at very low additional cost. Johnson & Johnson's Health Channel on YouTube started this way. Rather than starting from scratch, the J&J team drew from a supply of pre-recorded videos. As of April, 2014, it has more than seven million views and 6,000 subscribers;

7.   YouTube videos are easy to distribute via other social networks and to embed on websites and blogs as mentioned above.

Don't Discount E-mail

E-mail is the oldest of the digital channels and one of the most effective tools in the online "direct marketing" arsenal. Every healthcare organization should communicate with its customers — and prospects — via e-mail, which has many uses, including:

- delivery of content such as disease and treatment information via newsletters to both consumers and physicians;

- improving adherence to medication and compliance with physician instructions via alerts and reminders;

- driving visitors to websites for more information or special offers.

In recent years, pharmaceutical companies have put more emphasis on e-mail marketing focused on consumers, patients, and especially physicians who are not as receptive to visits from live sales representatives as they used to be.

Before implementing an e-mail campaign as part of your digital marketing strategy, it is important to understand the risks and learn from the mistakes of others.

The most important issues confronting e-mail marketers are privacy, security, and spam. It is not necessary to recount here all the recent security breaches that involve e-mail. Obviously, your e-mail campaigns will be more effective if you develop and implement best practices that protect the privacy of consumers and physicians, keep their personally identifiable information secure, and distinguish your e-mail from spam.

No pharmaceutical company has had more experience with security problems than Eli Lilly, a pharmaceutical company based in Indiana, that manufactures, markets, and sells several drugs, including the anti-depressant medication Prozac. In 2001, an inadvertent e-mail message led to Lilly becoming the first major pharmaceutical company to settle an online consumer privacy complaint with the FTC.[8]

From March 15, 2000 until June 22, 2001, Lilly offered to consumers the "Medi-messenger" e-mail reminder service. Consumers who used Medi-messenger could design and receive personal e-mail messages to remind them to take or refill their medication. Once a consumer registered for Medi-messenger, the reminder messages were automatically e-mailed from Lilly to the subscriber at the e-mail address she or he had provided, and according to the subscriber's requested schedule. These reminders were individualized e-mails and did not identify any other subscribers to the service.

On June 27, 2001, a Lilly employee created a new computer program to access Medi-messenger subscribers' e-mail addresses and sent them an e-mail message announcing the termination of the Medi-messenger service. The June 27 e-mail message included all of the recipients' e-mail addresses within the "To:" line of the message, thereby unintentionally disclosing to each individual subscriber the e-mail addresses of all 669 Medi-messenger subscribers.

According to the FTC's complaint, Lilly claimed that it employs measures and takes steps appropriate under the circumstances to maintain and protect the privacy and confidentiality of personal information obtained from or about consumers through its Prozac.com and Lilly.com websites. For example, Lilly's privacy policies included statements such as, "Eli Lilly and Company respects the privacy of visitors to its Web sites, and we feel it is important to maintain our guests' privacy as they take advantage of this resource."

Paraphrasing a line in a memorable Seinfeld TV episode, "You may know how to obtain sensitive consumer information, but do you know how to keep it secure?" That's really the most important part of the privacy commitment to your customers and essential for any e-mail marketing campaign.

Lilly has implemented a security program to comply with the FTC decree. This four-point program, which should serve as a model for all pharmaceutical and healthcare companies and their agents, requires Lilly to:

1. designate appropriate personnel to coordinate and oversee the program (that is, a privacy officer or someone with privacy officer responsibilities);

2. perform a risk analysis to identify internal and external security risks, including "any such risks posed by lack of training;"

3. through 2020, conduct a yearly annual written review to monitor and document compliance with the program;

4. adjust the program in light of any findings and recommendations resulting from reviews or ongoing monitoring, and in light of any material changes to Lilly's operations that affect the program.

There are many US and EU privacy laws and regulations impacting e-mail marketing. You should be fully aware of these laws and comply with them to avoid legal issues.

Aside from protecting customers' privacy, e-marketers must also distinguish their commercial e-mail from "spam," which is defined as "unsolicited commercial e-mail." Some studies suggest that as much as 87 percent of all e-mail messages are spam. Surprisingly, however, these studies have found that while there may be more spam, it bothers people less, perhaps because more of it is getting filtered and never reaching peoples' inboxes. You don't want that to be the fate of your e-mail messages. There will always be consumers who perceive ALL commercial messages as spam. As a consequence, some consumers may block your e-mail messages using spam filters or, worse, may lodge a complaint with the FTC. As the Lilly case demonstrates, it only takes one disgruntled e-mail recipient to initiate a suit and tarnish your public reputation.

Best E-mail Marketing Practices

To ensure the success of your e-mail marketing efforts it is critical to implement an e-mail marketing best practices program. Many best practice principles for composing e-mail marketing messages have been codified in the US CAN-SPAM ("Controlling the Assault of Non-Solicited Pornography and Marketing") law, which became effective January 1, 2004.

As a first step, marketers should practice "permission-based" e-mail marketing. This simply means that consumers, patients, and physicians must first "opt-in" or give their permission for the marketer to communicate with them via e-mail. Consumers can opt in via websites, call centers, or via business reply cards. Usually the permission is given in exchange for a perceived benefit such as a discount coupon, free newsletter, or participation in a compliance program. In the US it is legal for marketers to send one "unsolicited" commercial e-mail message, which can be used to secure opt-in for receiving further messages. Check, however, state laws.

Permission must also be revocable at any time. This is usually referred to as "opting out." This will be discussed in more detail below.

Some companies employ a corporate-level "blanket opt-in" option through which the consumer can opt-in to receive information about all the products offered by the company. This is seldom beneficial to the consumer unless the products are related. With a blanket opt-in the frequency of e-mail increases and the consumer is more likely to consider the sender a spammer. Frequent e-mail also may cause recipients to opt-out from further communication. It is much better to solicit opt-ins for specific purposes and limit your communication to fulfill those specific requests.

Spammers typically falsify e-mail headers to make it impossible to trace the source of the e-mail. Header information is usually not visible to the recipient of e-mail messages. It contains information, however, that e-mail servers use to route messages to and from computers. By using valid headers, you have taken the first step to distinguish your e-mail from spam.

For our purposes, it is enough to say that the "From," "To," and routing information—including the originating domain name and email address—should be accurate and identify the person who initiated the e-mail. Your company "initiates" the e-mail whether it "sends" the message itself or hires a third party.

All e-mails should be sent from a legitimate, active e-mail address. Replies should go to an inbox that is monitored in order to process opt-out and other requests.

To ensure the success of your e-mail marketing efforts it is critical to implement an e-mail marketing best practices program.

CAN-SPAM requires that commercial e-mail be identified as an advertisement and includes the sender's valid physical postal address. Your message should contain a clear and conspicuous notice in the body of the e-mail that the message is an advertisement or solicitation and that the recipient can opt-out of receiving more commercial e-mail from you.

Recipients of your e-mail marketing messages may not remember signing up to receive such communication from you. Consequently, experts recommend that a reminder be included at the top of each e-mail message informing recipients that they have signed up for the service. Also, be sure to direct recipients to the opt-out instructions, which should be included at the end of each message.

An example of this reminder might be: "You are receiving this e-mail communication because you requested this information. If you prefer not to receive future messages from us, please follow the instructions at the bottom."

Spammers frequently use deceptive subject lines to fool recipients into opening their messages. All e-mails should have accurate subject lines that do not mislead recipients about the contents or subject matter of the message. "ADV:" or "Advertisement" is not required to be included in the subject line.

This is probably a "no brainer" for most e-mail marketers in the healthcare industry. However, unless there is a standard procedure for reviewing subject lines, an enthusiastic marketing associate at your agency may insert a "cute" subject line designed more to improve open rates than to convey the contents of the message.

CAN-SPAM requires that each commercial e-mail message include instructions for opting out. You must provide a return e-mail address or another Internet-based response mechanism that allows a recipient to opt out of future e-mail messages. You must honor these requests within ten business days. You may create a "menu" of choices to allow a recipient to opt-out of certain types of messages, but you must include the option to end any commercial messages from the sender.

Provide a valid return e-mail address or a link to a website that allows recipients to unsubscribe (opt-out) from future e-mail messages. If you used multiple levels of opt-in, you should provide a "menu" of choices that allows recipients to select the types of messages they do not wish to receive (selective opt-out). In any case, you must include the option to opt-out from all e-mail communication from the sender.

Finally, do not sell or transfer the e-mail addresses of people who have opted out, even in the form of a mailing list, unless you transfer the addresses so another entity can comply with the law. For example, if you use multiple lists from various third-party sources, you should maintain a "suppression file" containing all the e-mail addresses of people who have opted out of receiving communication from you. You must provide this suppression list to the third party to "scrub" or remove the opt-out e-mail addresses from their lists.

This process can be quite complicated if you have recipients who have opted in for different kinds of communication and who subsequently opted out from one or another, but not all communication. A responsible third-party e-mailer should be able to handle this for you.

"Tele-Detailing"

According to the spring 2014 AccessMonitor™ report from global sales and marketing consulting firm ZS Associates,[9] only 51 percent of US physicians/

prescribers now allow access to pharmaceutical sales reps, down from 55 percent in 2013. Pharmaceutical companies have responded by ramping up so-called "non-personal" communication channels such as e-mail and live online chats to communicate with physicians on their own terms and times.

At an industry conference, Andrew Watson, VP of Sales & Marketing at Wockhardt USA, spoke about his personal experience using vRep, a virtual face-to-face selling application that allows virtual pharma reps to build the same type of relationships with doctors that traditional reps can. According to data presented by Watson, 70 percent of doctors are open to receiving virtual sales calls.

Eli Lilly in Italy has used "TeleWeb e-Detailing" or "Tele-Detailing," which involves a remote call made simultaneously by Internet and phone. A TeleWeb pharma sales rep makes an appointment by phone or e-mail with a doctor (or other HCP) who is invited to connect to a secure Internet site at a time of the doctor's choice. Once connected, the doctor is then guided by the sales rep who navigates for the doctor and comments on the content of the web pages via the phone line. The sales rep and the doctor see on their individual screens the same information (text, images, animations, videos, and so on) at the same time.

Mark Gleason, currently COO at Direct Medical Data, emphasizes that the combination of audio and web visuals—including videos—are key to improving retention. "Many years of tele-detailing have shown that audio is not sufficient for covering complex clinical data," said Gleason. "Adding the interactive web visuals has led to 8–10 minute interactions for PCPs [primary care physicians] and about 15 minutes for specialists. It also allows the rep to be a 'concierge' and bring up additional services like eSampling, patient educational material downloads, and links to other online video presentations."[10]

After TeleWeb calls, 60 percent or 70 percent of doctors are able to recall the key messages, whereas normally with in-person calls, only 15 percent to 20 percent of doctors can recall the key messages.[11]

Mobile Optimization

Meanwhile, the Search Agency reported that by the end of 2013, more than 26 percent of the health industry's Paid Search click share was coming from mobile devices; that is, smartphones and tablets.[12] And according to the 2014 US Mobile App Report by Comscore,[13] US "digital consumers" now spend more time using mobile apps than they do on desktop computers. This means that whatever your digital strategy is, you must remember that more often than not, consumers and physicians will be accessing your digital communication—tweets, websites, Facebook pages, and so on—via their mobile devices. At the very least, therefore, your website MUST be mobile-friendly and load quickly on mobile devices.

This means that drug and other healthcare companies would be better off optimizing their websites for mobile access than putting money into the development, distribution, and support of mobile apps. According to Klick Health, which is in the business of optimizing websites for mobile, "Google recently reported that 1 in 5 searches on Google are now from a mobile device. [Google] also asserted that ranking priority within mobile search results will be given to sites that are mobile optimized. This further underlines the need to ensure your website is optimized for mobile."[14]

Google took a deeper look at users' expectations and reactions toward their site experiences on mobile. "Most interestingly," said Google, "61 percent of people said that they'd quickly move onto another site if they didn't find what they were looking for right away on a mobile site. The bottom line: Without a mobile-friendly site you'll be driving users to your competition. In fact, 67 percent of users are more likely to buy from a mobile-friendly site, so if that site's not yours, you'll be missing out in a big way."[15]

In 2011, Google estimated that 21 percent of pharma sites are mobile-optimized. No doubt this situation has improved since 2011.

Even if your website is "mobile optimized," there are a few things to consider to ensure it is "mobile friendly." Here are a few suggestions:

- if you display a phone number, physical or e-mail address, make sure it triggers a call, e-mail, or directions when clicked on a mobile device;

- animations, video and other multimedia assets must be able to function without Flash support if you wish them to be visible on iPhones and iPads;

- many mobile users may not have a fast network connection. Make sure images are sized appropriately to load quickly over mobile connections;

- navigation must be "thumb" friendly with large click areas.

Mobile

Successful mobile strategies leverage the channels that are most compatible with audiences' characteristics and available resources, according to a pharmaceutical marketing study by Cutting Edge Information. The study, "Pharmaceutical Mobile Health: Transforming Brand Marketing, Healthcare Communication and Patient Adherence,"[16] found that pharmaceutical and medical device companies need to understand each mobile platform's benefit to optimize their channel usage and, ultimately, their mobile strategy. The findings also apply to other healthcare organizations.

Without a mobile-friendly site you'll be driving users to your competition.

For example, mobile phones in developing regions are unlikely to have capabilities beyond SMS messaging. Therefore, companies targeting sufferers of communicable diseases in developing countries, for example, should develop strategies aimed at the widely available SMS platforms first.

Findings from the mHealth study reveal that companies also need to dispel one-size-fits-all approaches when developing comprehensive mobile strategies. Within a mobile campaign that targets users attempting to quit smoking, for instance, text-based reminder initiatives may prove beneficial for some audiences but may not reach others. Instead, other users within the targeted group may benefit from a gamification platform or an information-based platform such as a mobile-optimized website. Given the variety of audience preferences, incorporating multiple channels to achieve a single objective is effective.

Mobile Apps

According to the Pew Internet and American Life Project "Mobile Health 2012" survey[17] on the use of mobile phones for healthcare, "half of smartphone owners use their devices to get health information and one-fifth of smartphone owners have health apps."

Healthcare marketers may assume that their digital marketing strategy must include developing a mobile health app—such as adherence reminders—for the 20 percent of consumers who have health apps on their mobile devices. But only about 9 percent of US adults over the age of 18 (19 percent of the 45 percent of smartphone owners) "happen to have" apps that help them track or manage their health. Keep in mind that "having" does not equate to "using"—we know from other surveys that the majority of these apps may have been used just a few times and then forgotten. Also, 81 percent of those 9 percent have health apps that focus on general health areas such as:

- exercise, fitness, pedometer, or heart rate monitoring (includes specific types of exercise like running, ab workouts, yoga, and so on)—38 percent;

- diet, food, calorie counter—31 percent;

- weight—12 percent;

- other "uses" include "period or menstrual cycle" (7 percent), "blood pressure" (5 percent), and WebMD (4 percent).

These types of "health" apps are very broadly focused and may not fit with your specific healthcare marketing objective. Pharmaceutical companies, for example, may find that there is not much interest among consumers for their brand-focused apps unless maintaining a healthy lifestyle is closely linked to the treatment. Many marketers of diabetes drugs, for example, have developed mobile apps for dieting, which is critical for supporting diabetes patients who take their drugs.

Still, competing with the many similar apps that are available to consumers is an uphill battle.

Apps are to be built around the needs of consumers and patients rather than around the companies' core products.

While some pharmaceutical companies have developed dozens of mobile apps, they have had limited success viz-a-viz downloads compared to other industries. One of the reasons cited for this is that the apps are built around the companies' core products rather than around the needs of consumers and patients.

mHealth App Quality Issues

In the early days of the Internet, hundreds of health websites of questionable quality proliferated without any guarantee of accuracy, lack of bias, privacy, security, or health information quality. Today, thousands of mobile health (mHealth) apps of unknown quality are available for downloading by HCPs and consumers and only 28 percent of smartphone users and 18 percent of tablet users report being "very satisfied" with the quality of available mHealth apps, according to a report from Booz & Company.[18]

To produce a high-quality mHealth app that truly meets the need of patients and that physicians will see as useful requires a really deep understanding of patient and provider issues. Innovative digital technology can help you obtain this kind of understanding cheaply and fast.

While most pharma companies say they are "patient centric," they will also tell you that it's too difficult to get feedback from patients. It's hard to find patients, takes too long, and costs too much. An innovative mobile research platform developed by Truvio, however, accelerates the process of obtaining the true voice of health consumers. The Truvio mobile platform, powered by the WEGO Health Activist Network of more than 100,000 opted-in and vetted consumer health influencers from more than 130 health conditions and topics, can collect informed patient opinions in real time.

Apps are to be built around the needs of consumers and patients rather than around the companies' core products.

Pharma Marketing News conducted a Truvio/WEGO Health patient poll in October, 2014.[19] WEGO Health patient activists were asked what the pharmaceutical industry could do to ensure that the mobile apps it develops meet the highest possible ethical standards and satisfy the needs of patients. Within hours, several patient activists answered this question and a few others, as well as provided audio comments via their mobile phones. It's a good example of how quickly a focus group of qualified patients can be tapped online. The results were very informative.

An asthma and allergy patient advocate, for example, suggested that there should be an independent diverse panel of people—a mix of doctors, patients, and pharma people—to brainstorm and put together "guidelines that are in everybody's best interest: the patients will be concerned about the privacy, the doctors will also be concerned about the privacy and the effectiveness of these apps and the accuracy."

A migraine patient advocate noted that: "Patient advocates have the patients' best interests at heart and know what patients would feel comfortable with and what they wouldn't. They would be the ones that would be familiar with what a person with a chronic illness is going to want in an application."

Some advocates suggested that patient advocacy groups such as the National MS Society, American Heart Association, American Cancer Society, American Lung Association, and so on, should develop guidelines for mHealth apps that "represent the patient's perspective, speak in the patient's voice, and accommodate patients' needs for quality mobile health apps."

See Chapter 2 for a few mobile health "Guiding Principles" that the healthcare industry should consider adopting.

Fabio Gratton, CEO of Vocalize, which developed Truvio, and creator of Pocket.MD which currently tracks over 6,000 industry-sponsored mobile apps, said:

> There is no question that we need some form of guiding principles for industry-sponsored mobile apps, but the unfortunate reality is that no amount of guides or principles can solve the issue of a poorly-conceived app. What I am seeing is companies creating apps that already exist in some similar form—and the rest are mostly brochureware mobile flip-books that never warranted a stand-alone app. While it's understandable that companies can make mistakes, what's not acceptable is not addressing critical issues after they have been reported with crystal clarity on the app store. It's really a shame that a company representative has not been assigned the task of reviewing comments and posting responses. It's really not that hard. In fact, Pocket.md offers a free tool that allows companies to receive alerts when comments are posted on their apps. This is one area where pharma could really rack up the karma points. Listen, respond, and optimize! [20]

Some Technical Issues

If you're thinking of developing a mobile application for patients or physicians, you need to consider the myriad platforms (hardware + software combinations) that are out there and determine which platform is best suited for your intended audience. Your choice of platform will impact your app's performance, maintenance, and security, which in turn will make or break the success of the app.

Google Android accounts for about 82 percent percent of the global smartphone market, ahead of Apple iOS (13.8 percent) and Microsoft Windows Phone (2.7 percent). In terms of tablet operating systems, the iPad share is about 50 percent vs. Android at 40 percent vs. Microsoft at 5 percent.[21] Which system does your audience prefer? Most physicians, for example, prefer Apple devices. About 70 percent of physicians use iPhones while 31 percent use Android-based devices.

The most obvious examples of mobile device diversity are screen sizes and aspect ratios. If you're designing a mobile website or mobile app to run on multiple platforms (even platforms using the same OS such as iPhones and iPads), it has to work on screens that range from tiny to huge. Aspect ratios also vary. A design that makes efficient use of a moderately-sized screen may just look goofy when scaled up to a much larger screen with a different aspect ratio.

The best place to start the decision process regarding what mobile platform is right for your app is to understand the intended audience. Perlman listed several questions about the audience you should ask, including:

- Does the audience use smartphones?

- What platforms have users embraced?

- How does usage deviate from the general population?

- How about tablets?

- Is there cognitive, visual, or motor impairment?

- If they are patients, do they rely on caregivers?

Sometimes, however, answering those questions isn't so easy. The following may be reasons why:

- too few users in population;

- multiple platforms preferred;

- data unavailable;

- immovable deadline precludes research;

- research was inconclusive;

- VP's kid likes Android, let's just go with Android.

The best place to start the decision process regarding what mobile platform is right for your app is to understand the intended audience.

Native vs. Web-based Apps

Perhaps further complicating the issue is the difference between native apps and mobile web apps. Native apps are downloaded and installed on the user's device (for example, iPhone apps downloaded from the Apple App Store). Mobile web apps, on the other hand, are accessed from a remote web server.

A mobile web app can work and look fine on a wide variety of platforms. Similar to a website that works with IE, Firefox, and Chrome on Windows and OS X, a mobile web app works with multiple mobile browsers across platforms. This is made possible by a technology called WebKit and the use of open standards. With some careful planning, a mobile web app written using these standards can support a huge cross-section of the market.

The downside of this "least common denominator" approach is that the app may not implement all the unique features of a particular platform, such as Apple's iOS multi-touch gestures.

Choose a native app when:

- you need access to the device hardware, such as the camera(s) or the accelerometer;

- you need to interface with external hardware, such as a blood pressure cuff or a blood glucose monitor or an autoinjector;

- your features must work without connectivity at all times, such as an app that provides information in an emergency scenario.

Choose a mobile web app when:

- you need the broadest platform support possible;

- you need to control the distribution channel;

- your users must have the latest content and features available for regulatory and/or legal reasons.

Social Media

So far we've discussed websites, e-mail, YouTube/video, and mobile as components of a comprehensive, integrated digital marketing strategy. Social media, which includes blogs, Facebook, Twitter, Pinterest, Tumblr, Wikipedia, and so on, must also be considered in your plans. Social media allow you to move beyond pushing messages out to a "target" audience and to engage the audience in two-way communication. Also, social media is how consumers and patients expect to access and interact with your organization and share your information with their friends, relatives, caregivers, and colleagues.

Before you embark upon a social media marketing campaign or consider it as part of your overall communication strategy, you should assess how ready you and your organization are with regard to social media marketing.

Over 1,500 healthcare marketing professionals have taken the *Pharma Marketing News* Social Media Marketing Readiness online questionnaire,[22] which helped them discover where they may need to augment their knowledge about social media and what internal legal/regulatory and cultural hurdles their organization may need to overcome to implement a social media marketing program.

The questionnaire asks the following questions:

Regulatory Environment (applicable only to companies regulated by the FDA)

- In your opinion, what is your company's general regulatory climate?

- There are a number of legal and regulatory issues associated with a drug firm's participation in or sponsorship of social media. How well do you and your colleagues understand these regulatory risks?

- How well do you think your company will be able to successfully address these compliance issues?

Corporate Culture

- What is your company's tolerance for risk (for example, initiating new or untested marketing tactics, launching bold corporate initiatives, and so on)?

- How does your company normally react to negative commentary from the media, physicians, politicians, and other stakeholders?

- How uncomfortable would your company be advertising in a publication or on a website that often contained editorial content critical of the pharmaceutical industry yet whose readers very closely matched your target audience?

Knowledge and Opinion of Social Media

- Rank your knowledge of social media in general—that is, how familiar are you with various forms of social media and how they are used?

- Rank your knowledge of how social media are impacting the pharmaceutical industry's customers and other stakeholders—that is, patients, consumers, HCPs, policy makers, and so on.

- Have you ever personally used social media (that is, read an online forum or posted a message to an online forum, submitted comments to a blog or written a blog post, edited a wiki, and so on)?

Compare your responses to these questions to those of survey respondents (see Figure 7.1).

A plurality of respondents (43 percent) from the pharma industry said legal/regulatory department was "very CAUTIOUS when it comes to taking regulatory risks and strive to avoid FDA warning letters at all costs." FDA released draft social media guidance documents in June, 2014, that might allay some of these fears, but pharma and other healthcare organizations—even those not regulated directly by the FDA—are wise to be cautious about the legal ramifications of social media faux pas. We'll talk more about that later in this chapter.

Being cautious, however, does not mean it is impossible to handle the legal/ regulatory issues that might arise. Only 7 percent of survey respondents said they do not have a good understanding of the risks posed by these issues and practically all (97 percent) of respondents think their organization can address some or all of such issues.

The best way to prepare your organization to handle the legal and regulatory risks of social media is to implement a social media policy to guide your employees on the use of social media, train your employees regarding the policy, and ensure that failure to abide by these policies will result in disciplinary action such as termination of employment.

Most healthcare organizations have such policies. The AMA in 2010, for example, adopted a policy to help guide physicians' use of social media. The Cleveland Clinic (CC) engages in conversations on the Internet via various social media platforms and has a set of "Employee Social Media Guidelines" as well as a "Social Media Code of Ethics,"[23] which states:

- Information posted on Cleveland Clinic web and social media sites, as well as information posted by Cleveland Clinic representatives on other social media sites will be accurate and factual. Cleveland Clinic employees will identity that they work for Cleveland Clinic and will disclose conflicts of interest.

- Cleveland Clinic will acknowledge and correct mistakes and welcomes feedback. When applicable, edits will be completed in a manner that allows tracking of changes.

- Cleveland Clinic will give credit to content authors and will provide direct online links when available.

- Cleveland Clinic reserves the right to remove content that is inaccurate, offensive or characterized as spam.

- When responding to certain individual posts, Cleveland Clinic will provide a name of a Cleveland Clinic representative, a phone number or email address for direct communication.

Roche Pharmaceuticals is one of the few drug companies that has publicly-available social media "principles" that advises its employees on using social media tools. These include rules for personal use when speaking "about" Roche and rules for professional use when speaking "on behalf" of Roche.[24]

Being cautious, however, does not mean it is impossible to handle the legal/regulatory issues that might arise.

Seven Rules for PERSONAL Online Activities

1. Be conscious about mixing your personal and business lives.

2. You are responsible for your actions.

3. Follow the Roche Code of Conduct.

4. Mind the global audience.

5. Be careful if talking about Roche. Only share public available information.

6. Be transparent about your affiliation with Roche and that opinions raised are your own.

7. Be a "scout" for sentiment swings and critical issues.

Seven Rules for PROFESSIONAL Online Activities

1. Follow the Roche Group Code of Conduct.

2. Follow approval processes for publications and communication.

3. Mind copyrights and give credit to the owners.

4. Use special care if talking about Roche products or financial data.

5. Identify yourself as a representative of Roche.

6. Monitor your relevant social media channels.

7. Know and follow our Record Management Practices.

Blogs

Before Facebook there were blogs, which consist of discreet entries (posts) typically displayed in reverse chronological order (the most recent post appears first). Readers are able to submit comments to each post and carry on a conversation about blog topics with other readers and the authors.

Many healthcare organizations, including pharmaceutical companies, now have blogs with posts written by their corporate communication department, affiliated physicians, and other staff, including marketing personnel. One of the first pharmaceutical corporate blogs was "JNJ BTW," which was launched by Johnson & Johnson in 2007. "Everyone else is talking about our company, so why can't we?," asked Marc Monseau who was then J&J's Director of Corporate Communication. "There are more than 120,000 people who work for Johnson & Johnson and its operating companies. I'm one of them, and through JNJ BTW, I will try to find a voice that often gets lost in formal communication."[25]

Like most pharma blogs, JNJ BTW accepts comments and its policy carves out what comments it won't publish: "We generally won't post comments about products that are sold by the Johnson & Johnson operating companies … comments that pertain to ongoing legal matters or regulatory issues are unlikely to be posted."

Aside from enhancing corporate communication, blogs can also be used to promote healthcare products and services. In 2007, GSK launched AlliConnect to promote Alli, its newly approved over-the-counter (OTC) weight loss pill. "GSK and the Alli blog folks are to be commended for this blog, which allows anyone to submit comments," said Pharmaguy. Alli marketers had to contend with "anal leakage" as a well-known adverse event. To meet the challenge, the Alli blog openly discussed the issue after recasting the problem as a "treatment effect." It also produced a YouTube video.

Online Message Boards and User-Generated Content

Online message boards are popular with patients (for example, PatientsLikeMe and Association of Cancer Online Resources) and even some physicians (for example, Sermo and Doximity).

Message boards typically consist almost entirely of "user-generated" content. Generally, each board is focused on a specific topic of conversation and visitors post comments and carry on asynchronous conversations via posts made to the board and replies to those posts. Blogs offer the same capability for conversation, but the original posts are written by the blog author and not by visitors/users.

> ## Aside from enhancing corporate communication, blogs can also be used to promote healthcare products and services.

The pharmaceutical industry has sponsored online message boards for a number of years. Some have even launched their own boards or purchased previously independent boards.

Prior to the launch of Alli in the US, GSK in 2006, for example, launched an online website called "Question Everything," which included a message board that was moderated by HCPs (for example, dieticians). Posts made to the board and responses from visitors and the paid moderators revealed how these discussions are mined for consumer insights and used to expand upon the marketing messages.

In June, 2012, Pfizer launched "Get Old," a multi-year initiative supported by nearly a dozen advocacy organizations. At the center of the Get Old initiative was a "first-of-its-kind online community" where people can "get and share information, add to the dialogue and contribute to the growing body of knowledge about this important topic," according to Pfizer's press release. The site allowed registered visitors to share their thoughts and experiences about getting old. Visitors were able to post links, videos, photos, or stories (including comments up to 1,000 characters) to the site. Visitors could also submit comments to other posts and "Like," tweet, or e-mail comments to friends. The site has changed to be less about UGC and more about messages from Pfizer and its partners. But it still allows comments to be submitted. "If it's truly awe-inspiring," says Pfizer, "we may use your comment elsewhere on the site."

What return on investment does Pfizer expect from its Get Old unbranded campaign? Obviously, it does not expect this effort to sell more drugs. However, Pfizer announced its commitment to develop drugs for medical conditions that afflict older people such as Alzheimer's disease. Soliciting UGC about getting old helps Pfizer understand the needs of people as they age. These insights are invaluable to its marketing campaign for promoting age-related drugs.

Facebook

Facebook has over a billion users worldwide, most of whom use the social media site to communicate with friends and relatives. It is also a great platform for healthcare companies to promote their products and services and interact with their customers and stakeholders. Mayo Clinic's Facebook page, for example, has garnered over 500,000 likes.

Pharmaceutical companies are also on Facebook. Boehringer Ingelheim (BI) posted a video on YouTube expressing thanks for the 50,000 people who have "liked" its Facebook page. The video features Allan Hillgrove, who is a member of BI's Board of Managing Directors, Division of Pharma Marketing and Sales. "Something has been cooking in the Social Media Lab here at Boehringer Ingelheim," said Hillgrove.

"Boehringer Ingelheim has been working hard to come up with a way to say THANK YOU for our over 50,000 Likes! We hope you enjoy this video we put together just for YOU!"[26]

Accumulating "friends" and "likes" on Facebook is not just a numbers game—it's a targeted advertising game. Most of the items in your Facebook news feed come from friends and sources related to pages and posts you "liked." Recent changes by Facebook allow for MORE text in the feed summaries. Bigger photos and more room for text are good news for pharma marketers who have struggled with complying with FDA regulations regarding "fair balance" when using online ad services.Healthcare marketers can take advantage of Facebook's new ad-friendly policies and target ads to people based upon their likes. Better yet, if consumers/patients "friend" your Facebook page—to download a coupon, for example—new posts to your page may show up in your friends' news feeds.

Up until August 15, 2011, companies had the ability to disable comments to Facebook wall posts, photos, and videos. This was called "whitelisting." After that date, however, Facebook no longer allowed whitelisting except in a few special cases. In other words, you must open your Facebook page to comments from visitors. It is critical, therefore, that you have a comment policy and allocate enough resources to manage comments (see below).

As a result of the new Facebook policy on comments, many pharmaceutical companies shut down their Facebook pages. Janssen Pharmaceutical, for example, shut down its ADHD Moms page, which was the first pharma Facebook page, launched in June, 2008.

Accumulating "friends" and "likes" on Facebook is not just a numbers game—it's a targeted advertising game.

"A new Facebook policy, scheduled for Aug. 15, will specifically impact communities that are formed to help people learn more about disease conditions, such as ADHD Moms™, which we sponsor," says a note on the ADHD Moms page. "This new policy will alter our ability to consider the appropriateness of comments before they are posted which is important to us as a company in a highly regulated industry."

Sanofi US, however, maintained its Facebook page, but noted, "To comply with applicable Laws and regulations, we do not use the standard Facebook wall for discussion." Sanofi does, however, allow comments on a special "Discussions" page where it previews them before being posted. "Just a friendly reminder that all posts are being moderated to ensure they comply with our Terms of Use," said Sanofi.

Other healthcare organizations such as hospitals, clinics, and physicians groups, which are not as strictly regulated as the drug industry, may be in a better position to deal with comments from users on Facebook as long as they devote the necessary resources to monitor comments (see below).

Twitter

When Twitter was first launched in 2006 many people wondered how useful a communication tool it would be considering that messages ("tweets") posted to Twitter were limited to 140 text characters. These days, practically every healthcare organization, many HCPs and patients, and ordinary people have Twitter accounts—some even have multiple Twitter accounts. A drug or other healthcare company may have a corporate communication account, a marketing account, a research-oriented account, and multiple brand accounts, not to mention mirror accounts in local markets around the world.

According to Twitter, there are 284 million monthly active Twitter users who send 500 million tweets per day. Interestingly, 80 percent of Twitter active users are on mobile and 77 percent of the accounts are outside the US. Twitter supports 35 plus languages.[27]

Twitter is a social network that revolves around the principle of followers. The tweets of people and organizations that you follow appear on your main Twitter page. You can also send personal messages (direct message or DM for short) to people who follow you and vice versa.

Twitter conversations or "TweetChats" about specific topics can be facilitated via the use of the # symbol, called a hashtag. Examples of hashtags used for health-related topics are #mHealth (Mobile health), #pharma (pharmaceutical industry), and #COPD (Chronic Obstructive Pulmonary Disease). You can find a list of more health-related TweetChats on the symplur.com site. We discuss TweetChats in more detailed later in this chapter.

Here's why hashtags are popular:

- People use the hashtag symbol # before a relevant keyword or phrase (no spaces) in their tweet to categorize those tweets and help them show more easily in Twitter Search.

- Clicking on a hashtagged word in any message shows you all other tweets marked with that keyword.

- Hashtags can occur anywhere in the tweet—at the beginning, middle, or end.

- Hashtagged words that become very popular are often trending topics that Twitter highlights.

There is a certain hashtag "etiquette" or best practice that you should observe. Twitter recommends:

- If you tweet with a hashtag on a public account, anyone who does a search for that hashtag may find your tweet.

- Don't #spam #with #hashtags. Don't over-tag a single tweet. (Best practices recommend using no more than two hashtags per tweet.)

- Use hashtags only on tweets relevant to the topic.

While the majority of "tweets" are text-only, it is possible to include images and video as well. In fact, such tweets are much more likely to be seen and read than pure text tweets. There are also many Twitter apps that make it easy to incorporate Twitter timelines (series of tweets) into your website or Facebook page.

A Twitter account can be used in many ways to support patients. The following are just a few options:

- drug/device safety alerts (for example, drug recalls, medical device malfunctions, emerging safety issues);

- prescription management, including pharmacy refill reminders;

- daily health tips from authoritative sources;

- publishing disease-specific tips;

- clinical trial awareness and recruitment;

- enhancing health-related support groups (for example buddy-systems for depression);

- providing around-the-clock disease management;

- patient-sharing of health-related experiences;

- issuing dietary/lifestyle tips;

- delivering adherence and compliance messages.

Although Twitter could be somewhat or very effective for nearly all of the patient-support activities listed, there are significant reservations about those activities that require personal communication such as disease management, prescription refill reminders, and patient stories. Obviously, it would not be acceptable to post patient-identifiable information to Twitter for all your followers to see. And DM'ing such information on a patient-by-patient basis may require use of Twitter technology that is not secure.

A Twitter account can be used in many ways to support patients.

Aside from supporting patients, healthcare organizations use Twitter to post messages of interest—whether it be health-related or general news about the organization—to other stakeholders, including physicians, investors, the media, politicians, and the general pubic.

TweetChats

We mentioned how hashtags can be used to organize discussions—"TweetChats"—around specific topics. Think of a TweetChat as a conference call using Twitter. The beauty of Twitter is that these messages can be broadcast to all of one's followers, rather than just linear correspondence between two people.

The privately-owned German pharmaceutical company Boehringer Ingelheim (BI) has hosted several disease-specific TweetChats focused on atrial fibrillation (#ChatAFib), chronic obstructive pulmonary disorder (#COPDchat), and lung cancer. Despite the regulatory challenges posed by such activities, these were all successful, both in terms of delivering value to stakeholders and to BI, while remaining compliant with existing laws and regulations.

Healthcare marketers can benefit from TweetChats by gaining insights as well as forging relationships with stakeholders who also benefit.

Healthcare marketers can benefit from TweetChats by gaining insights into the challenges of diseases and other subjects of the hosted chats as well as forging relationships with stakeholders who also benefit. Here are a few of the benefits of TweetChats that BI identified in its playbook titled *How Pharma TweetChats Can Drive Healthcare Innovation*:[28]

- Patient advocacy groups have the opportunity to share their first-hand experience of working with patients and providers with organizations that can act to improve disease management, but who may not fully understand the challenges being faced on the front line.

- Healthcare providers in turn can respond to the feedback procured from patient advocacy groups and patients around their challenges beyond the clinic and also escalate areas of unmet need to pharmaceutical companies and other providers of health solutions.

- Pharmaceutical companies procure real-life insight from both groups around the key areas of unmet need and how medicines, diagnostics, and broader support services need to address these. In addition, through facilitating these TweetChats, closer relationships are forged which can lead to further discussion and partnership beyond the confines of Twitter.

BI's playbook provides detailed insights for planning and delivering successful TweetChats. Successful planning begins with defining the topic and audience and deciding the right time to host the chat. For example, you might want to host the chat during an event such as a medical conference that covers the same or related topic. You should also plan for handling contingencies that may arise during the chat and be sure that senior management is on board and is well aware of the potential risks as well as the benefits.

Healthcare marketers can benefit from TweetChats by gaining insights as well as forging relationships with stakeholders who also benefit.

You should also promote the TweetChat in advance by inviting key participants and setting up an online "hub page," which includes details of the discussion topic, identifies the appropriate audience, specifies the "official" hashtag, and sets the date and time of the live chat. Advertise the chat and provide links to the hub page via Twitter. It is also recommended that you register the TweetChat hashtag with the Healthcare Hashtag Project (Symplur). This makes it easier for users to find the chat and access a transcript afterward.

The success of TweetChats cannot be measured using simple financial return on investment (ROI) metrics. Instead, consider the level of engagement such as the number of participants, number of tweets and the number of "impressions." Symplur determines the number of impressions by taking the number of tweets per participant and multiplying it with the number of followers that participant currently has. This is done for all participants during a specified time period. Finally, all the numbers are added up.

More engagement with stakeholders can lead to closer collaboration and health solutions that are of value to healthcare companies, providers, and patients.

Finally, TweetChats should not be seen as standalone activities. They should be integrated with the way your organization communicates via other channels.

To Moderate or Not Moderate

If your organization hosts a chat via Twitter, publishes a blog, owns an online message board, Facebook page, or a YouTube channel, it is important that you have a moderation strategy designed to meet your specific goals for that social media platform.

Generally, there are three social media moderation policies you could adopt:

1.   NO screening/moderation at all;

2.   pre-screening comments BEFORE they are posted;

3.   post-screening comments AFTER they are posted.

Although unmoderated discussion is the "essence of social media," unmoderated user-generated comments submitted to your company's social media site can potentially cause legal and/or public relations problems and promulgate misinformation that could be harmful to users. The pharmaceutical industry, for example, worries about adverse drug events and "off-label" information that may be posted to its sites. In the case of adverse events, companies are either legally or morally required to monitor or respond to those comments and report them to regulatory authorities.

In 2010, a disgruntled patient, Shirley Ledlie, flooded the VOICES Sanofi–Aventis Facebook page with comments about her adverse reactions to treatment with Taxotere for breast cancer. VOICES was a corporate communication effort to "[e]mpower employees, retirees, friends, families and communities to educate, engage, and mobilize with our grassroots network as we focus on healthcare industry priorities."

... it is important that you have a moderation strategy designed to meet your specific goals for that social media platform.

Ms. Ledlie suffered permanent hair loss during the course of her treatment. "This is my disfigurment from your drug Taxotere, the drug you kept this adverse side effect secret," she posted to the site's wall. "Why don't you want to answer my letters and emails?"

The VOICES Facebook page allowed unmoderated comments and lacked a Terms of Use notice or statement such as, "This site is not intended as a forum for discussing specific products or other treatments. It's best to talk to your doctor about specific treatments. You may want to contact our Medical Information Department for product specific questions at 1–800-xxx-xxxx."

Most experts agree that pre-screening comments BEFORE they are posted is the best option. The advantage of pre-screening is that it prevents misinformation from being published and then possibly propagated throughout the Internet. It also keeps the site from being overrun by spam or other malicious posts.

Pre-screening, however, requires significant resources in terms of monitoring and responding in a timely fashion considering the 24/7 nature of

Most experts agree that pre-screening comments BEFORE they are posted is the best option.

online discussions. You may consider an outside agency to do this work on your behalf, although you should read all comments submitted to learn more about the needs of your community.

Employ the correct mix of channels

Notes

1   Fox, S. and Duggan, M., Health Online 2013, PEW Internet Project [online]. Available at http://www.pewinternet.org/files/old-media/Files/Reports/PIP_HealthOnline.pdf [Accessed 8 January 2015].

2   Building a Best-in-Class Pharma Global Brand Website, Best Practices, LLC [online]. Available at http://www.prnewswire.com/news-releases/building-a-best-in-class-pharma-global-brand-website-300012750.html [Accessed 8 January 2015].

3   Mack, J., YouPharma: New Rules for Pharma Marketing and Social Media, *Pharma Marketing News* [online]. Available at http://www.news.pharma-mkting.com/pmn64-article04.pdf [Accessed 8 January 2015].

4   The Digitally Empowered Patient, Makovsky Health [online]. Available at: http://www.makovsky.com/insights/blogs/m-k-health/44-insights/blogs/m-k-health/732-the-digitally-empowered-patient [Accessed 15 April 2015].

5   Berstein, M., Searching for Answers on Search Engine Marketing?, *Pharma Marketing News* [online]. Available at http://www.news.pharma-mkting.com/pmn35-article01.pdf [Accessed 8 January 2015].

6   YouTube—The 2nd Largest Search Engine (Infographic) [online]. Available at: http://www.mushroomnetworks.com/infographics/YouTube---the-2nd-largest-search-engine-infographic [Accessed 8 January 2015].

7   Halper, R., Creating Compelling Video Content, Slide #4 [online]. Available at: http://www.slideshare.net/rhalper/exl-pharma-halperfinalrv21122 [Accessed 8 January 2015].

8   Mack, J., E-mail Marketing Best Practices for Pharma, *Pharma Marketing News* [online]. Available at http://www.news.pharma-mkting.com/pmn44-article01.pdf [Accessed 8 January 2015].

9   ZS Associates, If Physicians Aren't Listening to Sales Reps, What Are They Listening To? [online]. Available at: http://www.zsassociates.com/Publications/Articles/AccessMonitor-2014-Executive-Summary [Accessed 8 January 2015].

10   Mack, J., Pharma Tele-Web e-Detailing, *Pharma Marketing News* [online]. Available at http://www.news.pharma-mkting.com/pmn106-article01.pdf [Accessed 8 January 2015].

11   Mack, J., Pharma Tele-Web e-Detailing, *Pharma Marketing News* [online]. Available at http://www.news.pharma-mkting.com/pmn106-article01.pdf [Accessed 8 January 2015].

12   PharmaGuy, US Healthcare and Pharma Ad Spending in 2014: Mobile vs. Desktop, *Social Media & Mobile News & Views* [online]. Available at http://sco.lt/6XNkMj [Accessed 8 January 2015].

13   Lella, A. and Lipsman, A., The US Mobile App Report, Comscore [online]. Available at https://www.comscore.com/Insights/Presentations-and-Whitepapers/2014/The-US-Mobile-App-Report [Accessed 8 January 2015].

14   Mack, J., Mobile Optimization Offers Better ROI Than Mobile Apps, *Pharma Marketing News* [online]. Available at http://www.news.pharma-mkting.com/pmn1110-article02.htm [Accessed 8 January 2015].

15   Mack, J., Mobile Optimization Offers Better ROI Than Mobile Apps, *Pharma Marketing News* [online]. Available at http://www.news.pharma-mkting.com/pmn1110-article02.htm [Accessed 8 January 2015].

16   Transforming Brand Marketing, Healthcare Communication and Patient Adherence, Cutting Edge Information [online]. Available at http://www.cuttingedgeinfo.com/research/marketing/mobile-health/ [Accessed 8 January 2015].

17   Fox, S. and Duggan, M., Mobile Health 2012, PEW Internet Project [online]. Available at http://www.pewinternet.org/files/old-media/Files/Reports/2012/PIP_MobileHealth2012_FINAL.pdf [Accessed 15 June 2015].

18   Mack, J., Patient Activists Demand Higher Quality Mobile Apps, *Pharma Marketing News* [online]. Available at http://www.news.pharma-mkting.com/pmnews1307-article01.pdf [Accessed 8 January 2015].

19   Mack, J., Patient Activists Demand Higher Quality Mobile Apps, *Pharma Marketing News* [online]. Available at http://www.news.pharma-mkting.com/pmnews1307-article01.pdf [Accessed 8 January 2015].

20   Mack, J., Patient Activists Demand Higher Quality Mobile Apps, *Pharma Marketing News* [online]. Available at http://www.news.pharma-mkting.com/pmnews1307-article01.pdf [Accessed 8 January 2015].

21   Smartphone OS Market Share, Q3 2014, IDC [online]. Available at http://www.idc.com/prodserv/smartphone-os-market-share.jsp [Accessed 8 January 2015].

22   Mack, J., Rate Your Social Media Marketing Readiness Survey, *Pharma Marketing News* [online]. Available at http://www.surveymonkey.com/s/Y7V5L2Q [Accessed 8 January 2015].

23   The Cleveland Clinic Foundation Media and Social Networking Policy, Cleveland Clinic [online]. Available at https://www.appd.org/meetings/2012SpringPres/WS29Handout2.pdf [Accessed 8 January 2015].

24   Roche Pharmaceuticals, Roche Social Media Principles [online]. Available at http://bit.ly/c9Kacn [Accessed 8 January 2015].

25   Monseau, M., Welcome to JNJ BTW, Johnson & Johnson [online]. Available at http://www.blogjnj.com/2007/06/welcome-to-jnj-btw/ [Accessed 8 January 2015].

26   Thanks to our 50k facebook Likes!, Boehringer Ingelheim [online]. Available at http://youtu.be/a13yBuW4cwc [Accessed 8 January 2015].

27   Twitter, Twitter Fact Sheet [online]. Available at https://about.twitter.com/company [Accessed 8 January 2015].

28   PharmaPhorum, How Pharma Tweetchats Can Drive Healthcare Innovation [online]. Available at http://www.pharmaphorum.com/white-papers/how-pharma-tweetchats-can-drive-healthcare-innovation [Accessed 8 January 2015].

Chapter 8

Digital Patient Storytelling and Peer-Influenced Marketing

JOHN MACK

The PREZISTA Zone by Janssen Therapeutics—a division of Johnson and Johnson—includes a series of animations that tell the story of Jacob, a young man who has just been diagnosed with a "chronic disease" (that is, HIV infection). Jacob's story is told through a series of seven animated clips that help illustrate and explain sections of the Patient Information sheet that accompanies the prescription medicine PREZISTA® (darunavir), which is used in the treatment of HIV. According to Janssen, this program is designed to "transform the experience of exploring this information online through digital storytelling and animation."[1]

Features include:

- A selection of eight animated hosts who serve as site guides and narrate the Patient Information.
- The story of Jacob, a man who has just been diagnosed with a chronic disease, told through a series of seven animated clips that help illustrate sections of the Patient Information.
    - in the first episode, Jacob attends a disease support group session and learns how PREZISTA works;
    - in subsequent clips, he visits his physician to learn about medicines that should not be taken with PREZISTA, and visits his pharmacist who reviews the possible side effects of PREZISTA.

"As a physician, I know from experience that people tend to learn in different ways, and that can pose different kinds of challenges for patients trying to educate themselves about their medications," said Bryan Baugh, MD, Medical Director at Janssen Therapeutics. "We designed The PREZISTA Zone to meet a variety of personal preferences for learning and interacting with online information."[2]

In an omnibus survey of 1,047 people, which was sponsored by Janssen Therapeutics, 60 percent of those surveyed agreed it would be helpful to review Patient Information in an animated version that can be viewed and listened to online.[3] Physicians, which are strapped for time, can have their patients view relevant PREZISTA Zone animations while attending other patients. Such educational aids not only save time and improve physicians' practices, they also improve patient education and hopefully patient adherence to treatment regimens.

"Now more than ever, we need to focus on making brands memorable and storytelling is the way to do this," advised Ash Rishi, Co-Founder and Managing Director of COUCH, in a LinkedIn post.[4] "Engaging consumers through the art of storytelling can enhance a brand's strategy more effectively," says Rishi. "Data gives credibility, but stories provide truth, what's more, your consumers are more likely to engage with stories that resonate with them. We are all in such a crowded marketing space, but now we are competing with super brands that fully incorporate the art of storytelling into their marketing."

"Market research shows that the sick are relying more on the recommendations of fellow patients, and less on the reputations of companies and endorsers, in deciding whether to seek treatment and what drugs to ask for, say pharmaceutical companies and their consultants," noted the author of a *Wall Street Journal* article.[5]

Many healthcare companies, including drug manufacturers, are tapping into real, authentic patient stories as part of their peer-influence marketing efforts. Real patient stories can be found on social media sites and online patient forums or they can be solicited from patients directly.

Patient storytelling, peer-influenced marketing is winning the praise of the advertising industry. Janssen's Simponi's "Cate" campaign, for example, won a Gold Award at the Cannes Lions Health 2014 two-day "festival of creativity" in healthcare communication, held June 13–14, 2014.[6] Simponi is a drug approved for the treatment of rheumatoid arthritis. According to McCann Health Australia, the ad agency who created this campaign, the film features a "typical RA person—female between 50 and 60."

There is some controversy, however, regarding storytelling in marketing: Should the stories be true patient stories or "typical" stories of real patients as in the case of Cate? In a presentation at the Lions Health festival, Dr. Rita Charon, author of "Narrative Medicine," said "Healthcare is for truthful, authentic, discovering accounts of self."

In a YouTube study[7] unveiled at the American College of Gastroenterology's (ACG) 76th Annual Scientific meeting in Washington, DC, researchers at the Cleveland Clinic Foundation analyzed the top 100 most viewed Irritable Bowel Disease (IBD) related videos for content, popularity, and as a source of patient education information. They found that while YouTube can be a powerful tool for patient education and support, overall IBD content posted on YouTube was poor. "Clinicians and their patients need to be aware of misleading information posted by patients or particularly by pharmaceutical companies who often post videos to make it seem like they are coming from a patient when in actuality it is a company advertisement," said researcher Saurabh Mukewar, MD.

Patient storytelling, peer-influenced marketing is winning the praise of the advertising industry.

"No doubt a story would be more convincing if it is true, and we can envision drugmakers discrediting any fake narrative floated by a competitor," noted a Fierce PharmaMarketing article.[8] "That's a PR problem in the making. But given all that DTC [direct-to-consumer] history of fake patients, one could make a case for 'typical patient' stories. Either way, it sounds like a conundrum drugmakers need to address up front rather than risk being blindsided by criticism."

Dr. Mukewar agrees that the Internet and social media can benefit patients and enhance their care. But Dr. Mukewar said his findings are concerning to him since IBD patients may get misleading information via YouTube that could be harmful to their health.

Pharmaceutical companies have been recruiting real "non-celebrity" patients and soliciting their stories via unbranded social media sites. J&J Lifescan's Diabetes Handprint, for example, was a website that encouraged visitors to write on their hands a word or phrase expressing their feelings about diabetes, and sharing the story behind it. Visitors were able to click on the "Sharing" button to see "Real Stories" of people with diabetes.

Most of the time, these stories do not mention a product name and are not considered direct-to-consumer (DTC) advertising. Consequently, they are not regulated by the FDA. Some patient stories, however, are featured in DTC ads in the US. Pfizer, for example, needed to convince consumers that Chantix—unlike other smoking cessation products in the past—actually works. Key to their strategy is the use of real patients in their TV DTC ads for Chantix.

As mentioned in Chapter 2, according to the "Guiding Principles for Direct to Consumer Advertisements About Prescription Medicines" published by the Pharmaceutical Research and Manufacturers of America (PhRMA), "Where a DTC television or print advertisement features a celebrity endorser, the endorsements should accurately reflect the opinions, findings, beliefs or experience of the endorser. Companies should maintain verification of the basis of any actual or implied endorsements made by the celebrity endorser in the DTC advertisement, including whether the endorser is or has been a user of the product if applicable."[9]

Ordinary patients, however, may not be "celebrities" according to PhRMA. So paid patient testimonials, such as those seen in Chantix ads, may not be covered by PhRMA's Guiding Principles, which are self-regulatory in any case.

There may be hundreds of patients out there on social networks who currently earn thousands of dollars from pharmaceutical companies to be spokespeople as part of online branded drug or disease awareness campaigns.

The US Federal Trade Commission (FTC) is well aware of the trend and potential abuse of using patient bloggers as paid spokespeople. On April 13, 2009, *Advertising Age* reported: "As part of its review of its advertising guidelines, the FTC is proposing that WOM marketers and bloggers, as well as people on social-media sites such as Facebook, be held liable for any false statements they make about a product they're promoting, along with the product's marketer."[10]

In October, 2009, FTC revised the guidance it gives to advertisers on how to keep their endorsement and testimonial ads in line with the FTC Act. Under the revised Guides, advertisements that feature a consumer and convey his or her experience with a product or service as typical when that is not the case will be required to clearly disclose the results that consumers can generally expect. In contrast to the 1980 version of the Guides—which allowed advertisers to describe unusual results in a testimonial as long as they included a disclaimer such as "results not typical"—the revised Guides no longer contain this safe harbor.

The revised Guides also add new examples to illustrate the long-standing principle that "material connections" (sometimes payments or free products) between advertisers and endorsers—connections that consumers would not expect—must be disclosed. These examples address what constitutes an endorsement when the message is conveyed by bloggers or other WOM marketers. The revised Guides specify that while decisions will be reached on a case-by-case basis, the post of a blogger who receives cash or in-kind payment to review a product is considered an endorsement. Thus, bloggers who make an endorsement must disclose the material connections they share with the seller of the product or service. Likewise, if a company refers in an advertisement to the findings of a research organization that conducted research sponsored by the company, the advertisement must disclose the connection between the advertiser and the research organization. And a paid endorsement—like any other advertisement—is deceptive if it makes false or misleading claims.

Celebrity endorsers are also addressed in the revised Guides. While the 1980 Guides did not explicitly state that endorsers as well as advertisers could be liable under the FTC Act for statements they make in an endorsement, the revised Guides reflect Commission case law and clearly state that both advertisers and endorsers may be liable for false or unsubstantiated claims made in an endorsement—or for failure to disclose material connections between the advertiser and endorsers. The revised Guides also make it clear that celebrities have a duty to disclose their relationships with advertisers when making endorsements outside the context of traditional ads, such as on talk shows or in social media.

The US FDA, which has jurisdiction over prescription drug advertising—and not disease awareness advertising, which does not mention drug names, has also warned pharmaceutical marketers about patient stories/testimonials that make "unusual claims." In a Notice of Violation letter to Lilly in January, 2010, for example, the FDA cited two videos supposedly submitted by patients who take ADCIRCA, Lilly's drug approved for the treatment of Pulmonary Arterial Hypertension (PAH).[11]

The patient videos present statements made by Adcirca users, "Traci" and "Carolyn" who make the following claims among others:

"I can walk, and stairs don't bother me [after Adcirca treatment] … Bending over used to make me breathless, picking up my cat used to make me breathless and it doesn't affect me anymore."

"Exercising and stairs and heat used to bother me and it didn't bother me anymore [after Adcirca treatment]."

"Promotional materials are misleading if they represent or suggest that a drug is more effective than has been demonstrated by substantial evidence or substantial clinical experience," said the FDA letter. "'Traci's' and 'Carolyn's' statements misleadingly imply that patients treated with Adcirca will greatly increase their walking time and distance (e.g., 'from ... five minutes ... to one hour,' 'spending all night at the mall,' 'now I am walking on the treadmill,' and 'walking along the beach'). These statements significantly exaggerate what was demonstrated in the clinical trials for Adcirca," said the FDA letter.

Aside from complying with the FTC, the FDA, and other relevant governmental laws and regulations, there are several "pitfalls" that must be overcome when a pharmaceutical company or other healthcare organization decides to use patient testimonials. Leaving aside the legal issues regarding content ownership, some of the more interesting hurdles to overcome for marketers are:

- finding the right patient;

- assuring authenticity/believability;

- controlling the conversation in live/social media venues;

- transparency (for example, revealing payment).

To help answer the many questions that are raised by using real patient testimonials and avoiding the pitfalls, *Pharma Marketing News* hosted an online survey that asked respondents their opinions of the use of patient testimonials in DTC and social media advertising, including what the benefits may be, the regulatory issues, and how it may evolve, especially with regard to use of social media.[12]

Survey respondents felt that complying with FDA regulations, controlling the conversation, and assuring authenticity and believability were the main hurdles to overcome.

"Keep it open and transparent, otherwise it's not a real patient ... most 'testimonials' as they appear to date are trite, dishonest and lacking authenticity," said an anonymous respondent who works for a pharma agency.

"Credibility is the key word here," said another respondent. "By ensuring that patient testimonials deliver a balanced story, drug companies can avoid potential pitfalls. It's also vital to ensure that patients speaking on behalf of the company's product are representative of the average patient and not a miracle patient and that there is complete transparency and disclosure that the patient is speaking on the company's behalf. This not only ensures compliance with FDA regulations, it's the only way to assure authenticity and engage the target audience. Agencies working in the pharmaceutical field must have the experience and confidence to impress this upon their clients. Failure to do so risks a double dose of failure, namely, a lack of audience connection and unwanted interest from the FDA."

Are patient testimonial ads and peer-influenced marketing as persuasive as many experts believe? Survey respondents were asked to evaluate the following claims regarding patient testimonial ads:

- depending on the condition, these ads are more likely to motivate viewers to visit a doctor;

- patient-endorsed brands are seen as having less dangerous side effects than similar drugs;

- patient-endorsed brands are seen as more effective than similar drugs;

- these ads are more believable;

- these ads are more likely to gain attention and cut through the "clutter;"

- these ads are more memorable.

Are patient testimonial ads and peer-influenced marketing as persuasive as many experts believe?

Although over 60 percent of survey respondents agree that ads with patient testimonials are more believable than ads without such testimonials, non-celebrity patients alone don't make healthcare communication more effective. People struggling with a chronic illness are much more likely to engage with messaging that they feel is both authentic and realistic. Patient testimonials can be incredibly powerful, but it is imperative that the patient presents a balanced story. Patients should not be utilized to overtly sell a product. They should be utilized to build a mental model of success linked to a product.

Real-person experiences have the most influence in a social media environment where peers can converse and develop a relationship with the person relating the experience. To date, pharmaceutical companies that have tried to implement such online patient communities have withdrawn from that arena due to a lack of guidance from the FDA regarding how to handle off-label and adverse event comments.

In 2010, for example, Janssen Pharmaceuticals in the UK launched the Psoriasis 360 Facebook page, which was part of a larger disease-awareness campaign. "We would like people to join our community on Facebook and share their experiences with ourselves and others," said Alex Butler, who at the time was the Digital Strategy and Social Media Manager at Janssen.[13] "They can also connect with us and follow the latest psoriasis and 360 community news on Twitter. Shortly there will also be a YouTube channel that has been set up with the primary goal of YouTube itself in mind—letting people touched by the condition broadcast themselves and share their stories with others, helping people to live better with psoriasis. We believe strongly that people should be able to share their views in an open a manner as possible for a regulated industry and the commenting policy reflects this attitude," said Butler.

Real-person experiences have the most influence in a social media environment where peers can converse and develop a relationship with the person relating the experience.

Sadly, Janssen Pharmaceuticals shut down its Psoriasis 360 Facebook page in 2012.[14] Janssen cited its inability to moderate posts made to the Psoriasis 360 wall, one-third of which "mention[ed] a specific drug by name, or talk[ed] about the efficacy of a particular treatment is (or its side effects)." In a statement published on the Psoriasis 360 Facebook wall, the "Psoriasis 360 team" said "we have found ourselves removing a larger and larger proportion of posts, stifling worthwhile discussions."[15]

In any case, patients have many online forums such as PatientsLikeMe in which they can share stories and engage their peers. Rather than competing with these sites, healthcare communicators might consider collaborating with these communities to recruit patient "social media ambassadors" aka online "patient opinion leaders."

Tell a compelling story

Notes

1 Janssen Therapeutics, The PREZISTA Zone, [online]. Available at http://prezista. com/prezistazone [Accessed 9 January 2015].

2 Johnson & Johnson, Watching, Reading And Listening: A New Way To Interact With Patient Information [online]. Available at http://www.prnewswire.com/ news-releases/watching-reading-and-listening-a-new-way-to-interact-with-patient-information-148667445.html [Accessed 9 January 2015].

3 Johnson & Johnson, Watching, Reading And Listening: A New Way To Interact With Patient Information [online]. Available at http://www.prnewswire.com/ news-releases/watching-reading-and-listening-a-new-way-to-interact-with-patient-information-148667445.html [Accessed 9 January 2015].

4 Rishi, A., Data Gives Credibility, Storytelling Provides Truth in Pharma, COUCH [online]. Available at https://www.linkedin.com/pulse/20140710155636–21705051-data-gives-credibility-storytelling-provides-truth [Accessed 9 January 2015].

5 Rockoff, J., Trusting Other Patients' Drug Advice, *Wall Street Journal* [online]. Available at http://www.wsj.com/articles/SB100014240527487035102045750856905383 93342 [Accessed 9 January 2015].

6 Staton, T., Fake Patient Story Wins a Real-life Marketing Award? Discuss, *Fierce PharmaMarketing* [online]. Available at http://www.fiercepharmamarketing.com/story/ fake-patient-story-wins-real-life-marketing-award-discuss/2014–06–18 [Accessed 9 January 2015].

7 American College of Gastroenterology, Social Media Has Role in Delivery of Healthcare but Patients Should Proceed With Caution [online]. Available at http:// gi.org/wp-content/uploads/2011/10/2011acg_Social-Media__FINAL-Oct-26.pdf [Accessed 9 January 2015].

8 Staton, T., Fake Patient Story Wins a Real-life Marketing Award? Discuss, *Fierce PharmaMarketing* [online]. Available at http://www.fiercepharmamarketing.com/story/ fake-patient-story-wins-real-life-marketing-award-discuss/2014–06–18 [Accessed 9 January 2015].

9 PhRMA, Guiding Principles for Direct to Consumer (DTC) Advertisements About Prescription Medicines [online]. Available at http://www.phrma.org/sites/default/files/ pdf/phrmaguidingprinciplesdec08final.pdf [Accessed 9 January 2015].

10 Pharmaguy, Consumer Opinion Leaders: Pharma's Secret Sauce for Social Media Marketing, Pharma Marketing Blog [online]. Available at http://pharmamkting. blogspot.com/2009/05/consumer-opinion-leaders-pharmas-secret.html [Accessed 9 January 2015].

11 Pharmaguy, FDA Blasts Lilly's PAH eCommunity Videos!, Pharma Marketing Blog [online]. Available at http://pharmamkting.blogspot.com/2010/02/fda-blasts-lillys-pah-ecommunity-videos.html [Accessed 9 January 2015].

12   Mack, J., Use of Patient Testimonials in DTC & Social Media Advertising Survey, *Pharma Marketing News* [online]. Available at http://www.surveys.pharma-mkting.com/Pat-testimonial-survey.htm [Accessed 9 January 2015].

13   Pharmaguy, Markets as Conversations: Can You Have a Discussion with "Psoriasis 360" on Facebook?, Pharma Marketing Blog [online]. Available at http://pharmamkting.blogspot.com/2010/10/markets-as-conversations-can-you-have.html [Accessed 9 January 2015].

14   Pharmaguy, Janssen to Shut Down Psoriasis 360 FaceBook Page Due to Lack of Commitment, Pharma Marketing Blog [online]. Available at http://pharmamkting.blogspot.com/2012/03/janssen-to-shut-down-psoriasis-360.html [Accessed 9 January 2015].

15   Pharmaguy, Janssen to Shut Down Psoriasis 360 FaceBook Page Due to Lack of Commitment, Pharma Marketing Blog [online]. Available at http://pharmamkting.blogspot.com/2012/03/janssen-to-shut-down-psoriasis-360.html [Accessed 9 January 2015].

Chapter 9

Measuring the Results of Your Digital Efforts

LETIZIA AFFINITO

Imagine you have recently concluded a digital campaign to grow the number of stent replacement surgeries for your hospital, and by working with the cardiovascular service line director, you've ascertained that surgeries expanded 8 percent over the course of the campaign. Excited and happy, you present your results to the management leadership team, with pride displaying the number of cardiovascular diseases conference participants, the number of callers to the call center who asked about stent replacement surgery, and the 8 percent growth in surgeries as a result of the campaign. The CFO, or CEO, or perhaps a physician, will ask, "How do you know the increase in volume came from your campaign? How do you know those patients wouldn't attended anyway?"

It is the final defiance to both online and offline marketing communication outcomes: "How can you tell?" The challenge is strongly related to the ultimatum given before a marketing communication strategy is undertaken, often by an internal client such as a service line director/business unit manager/ CEO, who might claim: "Whenever you can't ensure this specific campaign will raise volumes 8 percent, then I won't support it."

Measuring success for their digital communication programs is a big challenge that health digital managers must now face. While it is important to get realistic metrics, it is, nevertheless, important to learn to view digital communication success in a more sophisticated and foresighted way.

Measuring success for their digital communication programs is a big challenge that health digital managers must now face.

Thinking of the problem simply in terms of financial returns would distort the ultimate value of digital and leave out the opportunities to meet a number of important outcomes. Measuring financial gains, while important, does not provide organizations with an exhaustive vision of an initiative's success or failure. It does not take into consideration how digital programs and applications improve targets' experience, for instance.

CLEVELAND CLINIC: COMMITTED TO HAVING STRONG METRICS BEHIND EACH PLAN

We'll begin our journey by going back to the Cleveland Clinic leading case history about digital marketing communication in action (Chapter 1). According to Paul Matsen, Chief Marketing Officer at Cleveland Clinic, his team creates 35 to 40 individual marketing plans for the organization's various hospitals and service lines and each plan comes along with a robust set of metrics behind it.

For example,[1] in addition to tracking national/local awareness and preference, Paul's team has a robust scorecard for digital that includes unique visits, online appointment requests (Figure 9.1), web requests (Figure 9.2), social media (Figure 9.3 and 9.4), My Chart[2] users (Figure 9.5) and web satisfaction. For its search engine marketing program, the team tracks the total number of leads generated, cost-per-lead, and return on investment (ROI). Standard metrics for media activity include the number of placements, their estimated value, and the tone—that is, whether the placements were positive or negative.

Having strong metrics is so important at the Cleveland Clinic that its marketing team also uses different tools to measure social media engagement relative to competitors' Paul Matsen says, "We don't rely solely on trying to measure ROI, and we don't excuse ourselves from measurement if we can't perfectly measure ROI. You start with what you can measure, then work your way toward a more complete measurement. And if you can get all the way to ROI, outstanding" (Beaulieu, 2012).[3]

Regardless of the importance of getting and analyzing metrics properly, according to a study by the Columbia Business School Center on Global Brand Leadership and the New York Marketing Association, 57 percent of CMOs and other marketing executives surveyed don't determine their budgets according to ROI measures. Sixty-eight percent of respondents said they base their budget decisions on historical spending levels, and 28 percent go with gut instinct. Moreover, more

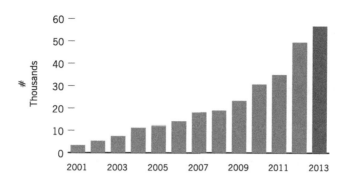

Appointment scheduling requests via the Internet reached 56,674 in 2013 — a 15% year-over-year increase.

Figure 9.1   Online appointment requests

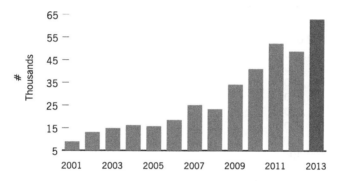

The number of people visiting and requesting additional information from our website and live chats continues to grow.

Figure 9.2   Web contact requests

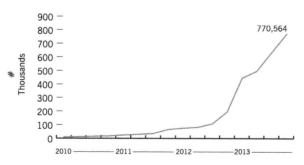

Increasing numbers of people are interacting with us through social media. Our rapidly growing number of Facebook fans now totals 770,564.

Figure 9.3   Social media—Facebook

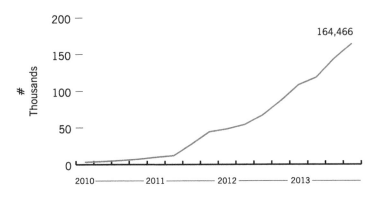

Twitter chats have proved successful this year. Our total number of followers has exploded to 164,466.

Figure 9.4   Social media—Twitter

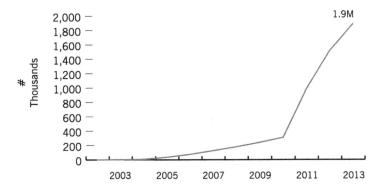

MyChart enables patients to have an active role in monitoring their healthcare. In 2013 all patients with an appointment were automatically enrolled in the application.

Figure 9.5   MyChart users

than half of respondents didn't include any financial outcome when defining marketing ROI (Beaulieu, 2012).[4]

Studies like these leave successful managers like Paul Matsen astonished, especially in today's bottom-line driven market. He thinks marketing people need to take responsibility for demonstrating the value of their function. "There are lots of tools to demonstrate the value of digital marketing efforts. We just need to learn and use all the tools we have to measure success," he said during an interview with Ken Beaulieu, Senior Director of Marketing and Communication, ANA.

"... We just need to learn and use all the tools we have to measure success, ..."

This is particularly true when referring to healthcare digital communication initiatives. Promoting health, in fact, is not just about rising sales. The ultimate aim of any marketing or communication initiative is to develop and strengthen a relationship with healthcare consumer to generate change and/or positive health behaviors.

In this chapter, after exploring some of the main ways to measure the success of digital communication, we'll explore some new approaches to analyzing healthcare digital campaigns results.

Before getting into the details of digital communication results measurement, it is important to premise that since, when measuring the comparative outcomes of a healthcare campaign one must surely deal with a range of variables, it can help, as a first step, to familiarize with all the variables that may possibly impact the outcomes of a digital marketing action. Some of them can be controlled and intentionally changed once you decide, for instance the marketing mix (for example, PR, advertising, social media), the duration of the digital marketing campaign, or targeted target demographic (supposing you can isolate segments, such as with a google ad campaign targeting only a certain gender). Nevertheless, there are some other variables which could be very hard or impossible for a healthcare communication manager to control, such as company brand awareness/perception/equity, competitive activity, overall economic conditions, and evolving customer characteristics, perspectives, and attitudes.

It would be hard enough for any communication manager to isolate even one variable under his/her control, but there is no possible way to control for all the variables. The very best one could do is to understand what variables are in effect with a given measurement over time and make many measurements hoping to understand the impact of the various variables on digital marketing results.

Anytime it is possible, you'd better set up a baseline measurement concurrent with your present campaign. A baseline measurement either looks at a earlier time period where there was no digital marketing communication effort or compares your marketing effort to the results from a similar target audience segment that wasn't exposed to your effort.

A good principle is usually that the further back in time you have to go, the less reliable your appraisal will be. Whenever possible, test and compare your marketing effort to a standard period a maximum of two years.

Behavior-Centric Approach to Digital Health Content Measurement

Given this premise, an acceptable approach to justifying investments in digital health content is behavior-centric, a premise which was first articulated by the innovation consultancy Enspektos, LLC.[5]

Enspektos suggests that quantifying the economic impact of digital health content investments on behavior can help in three main ways:

- ensuring that digital communication initiatives are measured based on their general economic benefits, not merely on organizational profitability;

Anytime it is possible, you'd better set up a baseline measurement concurrent with your present campaign.

- encouraging strategic focus on digital health content;

- encouraging extensive adoption of digital technologies within the health industry.

Enspektos goes on to suggest the health industry adopt a metric it created in 2012 called "Return on Health Behavior" or ROhB, which measures the aggregate short- and long-term economic value associated with activating and sustaining positive health behaviors via digital health content.

According to Enspektos, ROhB's benefits include the following:

- *ROhB recognizes the new financial reality*: it quantifies how the economic benefits of digital health content flow between organizations and society.

- *Both the public and private sectors can use ROhB*: it allows the public and private sectors to speak the same language when quantifying digital health content's benefits;

... an acceptable approach to justifying investments in digital health content is behavior-centric ...

- *ROhB encourages innovation*: it can help justify experimental or long-term investments. Positive ROhB = worthwhile activity.

In addition to the ROhB metric, Enspektos developed a framework called the "Health Behavior Levels Matrix" (Figure 9.6) to outline the types of behavior which digital health content can activate or sustain. The Matrix presents four levels of behavior:

Level I: Engagement or activity behaviors commonly associated with consumption of online health content. These can include watching videos or sharing a Twitter post.

Level II: Purchase or donation behaviors activated by online health content, including decisions to seek or prescribe medication or donate to a cause.

Level III: Short-term health behaviors which do not require a long-term commitment such as getting screened for heart disease or being vaccinated.

Level IV: Long-term health behaviors which require a significant commitment such as taking medication for life or maintaining an exercise program.

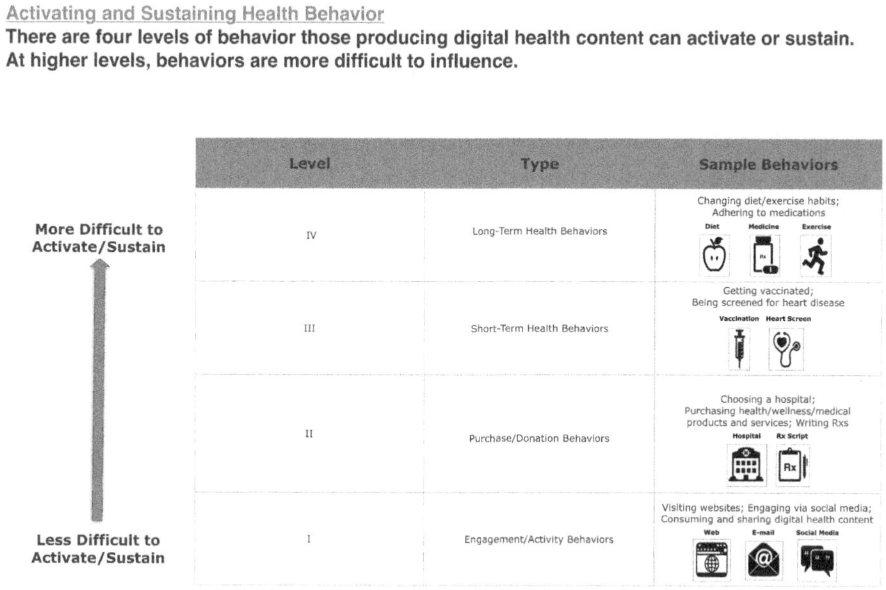

Activating and Sustaining Health Behavior

There are four levels of behavior those producing digital health content can activate or sustain. At higher levels, behaviors are more difficult to influence.

Figure 9.6   Health Behavior Levels Matrix

Source: Enspektos.

Additional information about how the system can be applied (as described by Enspektos, in its publication *Justifying the Digital Health Content Investment*), is outlined below.

USE WEB AND SOCIAL ANALYTICS TO MEASURE LEVEL I BEHAVIORS

As outlined by Enspektos, the first goal of any digital health content initiative is to drive awareness and engagement. Level I of the Matrix accounts for these behaviors. These can be measured using a range of technology, as described below.

- *Web Analytics*: Web analytics platforms can provide a wealth of information about how people arrive at and consume health content on a website. This data can also be used to examine the types of content that improve awareness and sales.

- *Social Analytics*: There are many technologies that reveal how people engage with (likes, tweets, retweets) and may perceive (sentiment) online content.

MEASURE LEVEL II BEHAVIORS WITH DIGITAL ANALYTICS, SURVEYS, AND CUSTOMER RELATIONSHIP MARKETING PLATFORMS

Ignoring sales, revenue, and profits is perilous, especially for private sector organizations such as pharmaceutical companies and hospitals.

Digital analytics and surveys can reveal how online health content is driving hospital visits and coupon redemptions. It can also help organizations properly attribute social media to increased revenues and profits.

In the case of surveys, asking people how they heard about an event or why they redeemed a coupon can reveal a lot about what is driving purchase behavior.

Customer relationship marketing (CRM) programs can be leveraged to provide a range of data on the following:

- *Acquisition*: How potential customers are acquired (via newsletters, web content or other means).

- *Conversion*: Which touch points (such as e-mail, events, white papers, in-person detailing, and so on) move people from consideration to purchase.

- *Social media impact*: Social media being used by customers and prospects, and which content drives online purchase behavior (clicks, likes, additional sales).

MEASURING LEVEL III AND IV BEHAVIORS: A NEW FRONTIER

Existing techniques and technologies do a good job of providing data on Level I and II behaviors. However, teasing out how digital content influences Level III and IV actions is more difficult.

The authors of Peel's literature review of health and social media tackled this question.[6] (12) They wrote: "When controlled research included an evaluative component, the results were often confounded by a failure to isolate the [social media] intervention from other communication strategies."

Clearly, measuring the behavioral impact of digital health content is a difficult task. However, as discussed above, doing so is critical.

Enspektos has acknowledged that many existing platforms fall down when it comes to measuring Level III and IV behaviors. Content activity, sentiment, and engagement data don't provide information about health behavior.

In the paid content arena, technology is more advanced.

However, much of the health content people consume online is earned, or non-advertising. How can we measure its performance? Enspektos has suggested that this is the next frontier in health behavior measurement.

Following are some key requirements for projects or technologies, as outlined by Enspektos, designed to tackle this problem:

- *Isolating digital inputs*: Analyzing digital inputs separately allows for direct comparison. For example, health content received via Facebook may perform differently than information posted to a blog.

Clearly, measuring the behavioral impact of digital health content is a difficult task. However, as discussed above, doing so is critical.

- *Accounting for offline effects*: Behavior is influenced by many factors. What is the relative role of online content versus offline influencers?

- *Controlling for motivation and ability*: How does content perform among individuals with high versus low motivation and ability?

- *Understanding the full digital environment*: People do not consume digital health content in isolation. What else are they seeing online? Does this information contain positive or negative messages? How is this content influencing behavior?

- *Right-time data*: Digital media is ever moving. Is data provided at the right time?

Mobile, Big Data, and Health Behavior Change

When it comes to measuring mobile marketing, most of the work is conducted to understand patients' real-world clinical outcomes. For example, data can be mined from social media channels to understand the following:

- what medication-related decisions consumers are making;

- why patients made these choices—for example, because of medication side effects or other factors.

Despite many advances, more work is required. First, many consumers in various health stages (pre-diagnosed, recently diagnosed, considering treatment, and so on) are not actively discussing their conditions online.

Second, the web is changing constantly. We need a better understanding of how ever-evolving digital information triggers influence the vast majority of people consuming rather than creating digital content.

This information can be used to help people:

- understand how individual pieces of digital content influence health behavior;

- provide the appropriate level of evidence required to accurately calculate ROhB.

Digital technologies will only grow in importance as patients, health providers, and other stakeholders embrace them. Because of this, health organizations will continue to invest in these tools.

But the private and public sectors will not be well served by simply focusing on the low-hanging fruit of digital measurement: revenues and content engagement.

We predict organizations that invest in demonstrating positive ROhB will be at a significant competitive advantage. They will be more likely to innovate. These organizations will also reap the economic rewards associated with consistently delivering effective and engaging digital health content.

Digital Communication Measuring Starts with Campaign Planning

Although some free computerized technology can offer health communication managers with a useful glance into their brands track and get an understanding of the social space, HCPs, pharma/biomedical companies, and marketers alike continue to seek an answer to the long-standing question, "What's my ROI?".[7]

The capability to address this question depends on the way the campaign was designed and if well-defined calls to action (CTAs) were included into the strategy.

We predict organizations that invest in demonstrating positive ROhB will be at a significant competitive advantage.

In order to accurately measure the ROI of a digital campaign it is important to execute the following steps:

- *Set up and agree on clear business objectives.* What is your primary objective? Create awareness on your product or service? Create demand? Educate patients on a disease? Offer patient support? Create patients loyalty?

- *Include hard offers.* Offering an appointment with a doctor (that is, "free consultation") as a part of the online experience (that is, as a benefit of taking part in the conversation) will offer a link to marketing information.

- *Define the KPIs.* Are you trying to increase the number of monthly visitors to your site? Or are you trying to create/increase patient engagement? Your KPIs should appraise performance aligned with the set business objectives.

Table 9.1 lists some recommended KPIs you could track regularly:

Table 9.1   Main key performance indicators

Website	Number of monthly unique visitors to your site (get this from Google Analytics) Time spent on site Goal conversion rate (if you have set up goals) Number of new blog posts
Twitter	Followers Number of tweets retweeted by others (there are also some tools out there like Tweet Reach which give better measures of impact)
Facebook page	Reach and engagement (from the Facebook Insights page)
E-mail newsletters	Number on mailing list Number of newsletters sent Average open rate Average click rate

The capability to address this question depends on the way the campaign was designed and if well-defined calls to action (CTAs) were included into the strategy.

Nevertheless, measurement should not stop here because, for example, it does not tell us what patients thought about the campaign in the case of a pharma company, or whether it has had an impact on physicians' clinical practice.

Data on the level of interactivity can truly help to ascertain if a campaign is creating value.

Data on the level of interactivity, such as degree of awareness and perception before and after a campaign, and changes in health behavior, can truly help to ascertain if a campaign is creating value. Organizations can use these insights to generate and keep significant levels of commitment among target groups of patients throughout the product/service lifecycle.

A rise in sales is, of course, the best accepted measure of success, but it can be very hard to exactly ascribe or relate investment in digital programs to quick increases in sales because digital activity measurement must include all the other activities that take a patient on a journey of awareness, interest, desire, and action.

Data on the level of interactivity can truly help to ascertain if a campaign is creating value.

Measuring the Effectiveness of Social Media

Most of the blog posts, whitepapers, and opinion leaders have recently focused on measuring the effectiveness of social media using soft metrics (also known as "buzz" metrics). These social brand metrics include units of measure such as:

- the amount of discussion happening (volume);

- the speed at which volume is increasing (velocity);

- the degree to which the conversations are positive or negative (sentiment);

- the perceived importance of who is talking and their influence over others (influence).

Sophisticated analytics programs offered by many marketing computerized platforms are designed to track each step of a digital marketing campaign, from lead generation to conversions to customer retention. The most difficult aspect of measuring digital communication results in healthcare is determining a timeframe by which to judge whether a positive return has been made. The only solution to this challenge is a comprehensive tracking system that takes into account all expenses and revenue.

Measuring Healthcare Pay Per Click

When implemented correctly, Paid Search advertising can offer a number of benefits to a healthcare organization. For example, it can allow healthcare providers to target a niche audience or increment the number of scheduled procedures. As a consequence, measuring pay per click results is valuable because it makes sure a healthcare organization, for example, spends its budget more profitably. It gives information about which areas you can improve upon. Through analytics, you can learn the following about your paid search campaigns:

- the location of your target audience;

- what ad messaging resonates with searchers;

- what landing page layout and elements convert visitors;

- which keywords yield clicks;

- what the core needs of your audience are;

- how effective Search Retargeting is for your campaigns;

- where you need to adjust and allocate campaign budgets to maximize efficiency and increase traffic/leads.

The most difficult aspect of measuring digital communication results in healthcare is determining a timeframe by which to judge whether a positive return has been made.

It is important to focus on the metrics that truly indicate how financially responsible your Paid Search efforts are. These include:

- cost-per-click (CPC);

- cost-per-lead (CPL);

- conversion rate (conversions/clicks);

- cost per action (site engagement: video tour, blog page visits, and so on);

- tracking URLs.

The meaning of a "conversion" will vary among healthcare organizations. For example, when promoting services, such as "lasik eye surgery," a conversion would probably require a visitor to call a trackable number to schedule a consultation.

It is important to focus on the metrics that truly indicate how financially responsible your Paid Search efforts are.

An organization like the American Diabetes Association, however, might consider a conversion to be filling out a form to receive an information packet.

Measuring Digital Content Results

The principal objective in content marketing is quality traffic to your site.[8] There is strong variance in the amount of traffic generated by different content marketing operations. Some consumer-focused brands have succeeded in generating high traffic volumes. Niche, B2B brands achieve more modest traffic numbers but meet their objectives by building a highly targeted audience. Content marketing involves moderate upfront expenses and low short-term financial results. Only after a number of months, as the operation begins to grow its audience and influence, does it begin to deliver cost-effective results.

As stated by Joe Pulizzi (2012),[9] "content marketing is not a campaign." Nowadays, marketers don't buy media, they become the media itself and, most of all, they don't pay for an audience, they earn an audience. As you may understand, these are both processes which take time.

The principal objective in content marketing is quality traffic to your site.

As a consequence, managers who start a content marketing program must understand that it is a long-term effort, requiring significant investments of time and resources before its results can be measured positively.

To ensure that investment produces the expected results, content marketing must evolve from an experiment to a structured business process. In addition, content marketers must measure the performance of their work so that they can constantly enhance their operation. Leadership needs insights into not only aggregate performance, but also performance analyzed by different dimensions such as author, category, and content type so that the team can understand what's working, what isn't, and why.

To ensure that investment produces the expected results, content marketing must evolve from an experiment to a structured business process.

Focus on behavior change

Notes

1   Cleveland Clinic State of the Clinic Annual Report, 2013.

2   Cleveland Clinic MyChart® is a secure, online tool that connects patients to personalized health information from the privacy of their home at any time, day or night. Cleveland Clinic MyChart also alerts patients to important, institutionally-determined health-related reminders to help them better plan the details of their ongoing health care.

3   Beaulieu, K. (2012), Delivering Measureable Results at Cleveland Clinic [online]. Available at http://www.ana.net/blogs/show/id/23249 [Accessed 18 November 2014].

4   Beaulieu, K. (2012), Delivering Measureable Results at Cleveland Clinic. Association of National Advertisers (ANA). [online]. Available at http://www.ana.net/blogs/show/id/2324 [Accessed 3 December 2014].

5   Enspektos LLC, 2012. Justifying the Digital Health Content Investment [online] Available at <http://enspektos.com/justifying-the-digital-health-content-investment/> [Accessed 18 November 2014].

6   Schein, R. et al (2010), Literature review on effectiveness of the use of social media – A Report for Peel Public Health – Toronto [online] Available at https://www.peelregion.ca/health/resources/pdf/socialmedia.pdf [Accessed 3 December 2014].

7   Pixels & Pills (2010), Effectively Measuring Social Media ROI in Pharma [online] Available at http://pixelsandpills.com/2010/06/01/effectively-measuring-social-media-roi-pharma/ [Accessed 3 December 2014].

8   Eloqua & Kapost (2012). Content ROI Marketing [online]. Available at http://marketeer.kapost.com/wp-content/uploads/2012/06/Content-Marketing-Kapost-Eloqua-eBook.pdf [Accessed 3 December 2014].

9   Pulizzi, J. (2012), Content Marketing is Not a Campaign. This is a Promise to Our Customers VIDEO [online]. Available at http://marketeer.kapost.com/joe-pulizzi-content-marketing-is-not-a-campaign-this-is-a-promise-to-our-customers-video/#ixzz3NQvFJQE1 [Accessed 3 December 2014].

Chapter 10

Crowdsourcing and Co-creating for a Patient-Centered Health Communication

LETIZIA AFFINITO

If one metric by which to determine the relevance of communication and marketing to public health practice is the extent to which they are capable of creating—or contributing to—beneficial changes in each of the five fields of influence synthesized in the People & Places Framework proposed by Maibach et al. (2007)[1] (see Chapter 1) and most people are driven by a need to influence the outcomes that affect their everyday lives (Edward Deci and Richard Ryan, 2002)[2] then crowdsourcing and co-creation can represent a very effective way to encourage communication among patients and between patients and health providers (both physicians and pharma/biomedical managers). If well planned and implemented a crowdsourcing or co-creation project may become an "innovative" way to engage patients and generate change while communicating a message that is, disease prevention) or a brand. In fact, as a significant part of a crowdsourcing competition/co-creation project it is crucial to focus on:

- developing the marketing campaign;

- developing and realizing events aiming at amplifying the message;

- planning an effective social media campaign.

The term "crowdsourcing," which was first coined in 2006, refers to openly soliciting ideas and solutions from different individuals, usually using the Internet.

These days, artists are crowdsourcing art, design companies are crowdsourcing designs, major brands are crowdsourcing television ads, start-ups are crowdsourcing logos, and expectant parents are crowdsourcing baby names. Yet, it may seem surprising that crowdsourcing and co-creation have also entered healthcare, a field featured by its accurate training requirements, high level of specialization, and infinite layers of regulation.

... crowdsourcing and co-creation can represent a very effective way to encourage communication among patients and between patients and health providers ...

Actually, the challenge currently faced by providers, pharma/biomedical companies, patients and researchers seems to perfectly lend itself to the collective, large-scale problem-solving model crowdsourcing and co-creation can provide to create value for the patient.

In this chapter we will explore what is crowdsourcing and co-creation, how they differ and how managers can use them to create patient empowerment and engagement to make them key players in the development of value-added health solutions aiming at improving their own experience. Finally we'll see how they can contribute to organizations' communication and branding.

Crowdsourcing in Action at PatientsLikeMe

We'll begin with a leading case history about crowdsourcing in action at PatientsLikeMe, the Cambridge, MA-based company, a provider of patient social networking communities, that received grants totalling $4.3 million from the Robert Wood Johnson Foundation to lead an effort that puts patients at the center of developing health outcome measures, which have traditionally been the domain of medical experts.

The "vast majority" of health outcomes are currently built to measure a single, quantifiable result across a population of patient. Almost none firmly reflect patients' experiences with a disease or evaluate health and quality of life in ways that are relevant to patients.

The new web-based Open Research Exchange (ORE) platform consists of a database of measures and instruments, an interface for aspiring authors, a community for communication and collaboration, and a tool providing access to the PatientsLikeMe database for the purpose of validating measures. The crowd system combined the "best elements" of Wikipedia, crowdsourcing website Quora, and Yahoo Answers, and will work on mobile devices.

The measures found ought to be longitudinally valid as well as expressive of patients' individual differences.

The long-term plan of PatientsLikeMe is to help the pharmaceutical industry develop a "global integrated [patient] registry across diseases," necessitating "robust [health outcome] measures." (Borfitz 2013).[3]

As PatientsLikeMe co-founder and Chairman Jamie Heywood tells, during an interview with Borfitz from *Bio-IT World*, the new approach to developing outcome measures from his company should lead to measures that reflect the things that are important to patients. This method of crowdsourcing for outcome measures comes amid efforts by others to tap the input of patients and others to improve clinical studies, including Transparency Life Sciences' FDA-approved study of an MS treatment designed with an online platform.

"What is novel about patient-reported outcomes is we are harnessing the best ideas for measuring each condition through a crowdsourcing, open-source approach. This will dramatically accelerate our understanding of human health," Heywood continues. "If we can create a shared partnership with patients and researchers, it will break down a lot of silos, barriers and cost inefficiencies so we can improve and increasingly use outcome measures as a de-facto practice."[4]

The company released a beta version of the new ORE platform in 2013. This effort garnered some interest from academic researchers, patients, and drug makers seeking new ways to advance new therapies that make meaningful dents against diseases, showing a willingness to listen to patients along the way. Merck and Novartis are among a dozen or so pharma groups with therapies targeting MS, ALS, transplants, epilepsy, cancer, and psoriasis that have already collaborated with PatientsLikeMe, and other drug makers have signed on with other tech outfits to gain information on what patients are saying about treatments (McBride 2013).[5] PatientsLikeMe presently sells knowledge of the real-world experience of patients based on a combination of measures over time, as well as predictive computational outcome models for MS and ALS patients.

At PatientsLikeMe, patients have been contributing data on their diseases for years and building data sets that pharma companies have used to inform their drug research. With the new ORE platform, patients have the opportunity to offer advice to their peers, to foster relationships based on shared attributes, and to collaborate on developing outcome measures that better evaluate the efficacy of new drugs, including elements that matter to those taking the medicines, that is patients.

> **At PatientsLikeMe, patients have been contributing data on their diseases for years and building data sets that pharma companies have used to inform their drug research.**

From Product-Centered Thinking to Focus on the Experiences That Customers Will Seek to Co-Create

The word "market" recalls two different definitions:

- an aggregation of consumers;

- the locus of exchange.

The concept of a market is changing and transforming the nature of the relationship between the consumer and the firm.[6] According to the traditional view, the market didn't take part in the value creation process.

Consumers were "outside the firm" while value creation took place exclusively inside the firm (throughout its activities).

With the increasing and fast advent of social media, consumers are no longer totally dependent on communication from the firm. They are now submitting the industry's value creation process to scrutiny, analysis, and evaluation (Table 10.1). Consequently, consumer-to-consumer communication and dialogue provides consumers with an alternative source of information and perspective.

According to Prahalad and Ramaswamy (2004) "consumers can choose the firms they want to have a relationship with based on their own views of how value should be created for them. High-quality interactions that enable an

Table 10.1   Moving customers

FROM	TO
Passive Purchasers	Active Representatives
Listening	Conversing
Consumers As Purchasers	Consumers As Resources

Source: Adapted from Prahalad and Ramaswamy, 2004.

With the increasing and fast advent of social media, consumers ... are now submitting the industry's value creation process to scrutiny, analysis, and evaluation.

individual customer to co-create unique experiences with the company are the key to unlocking new sources of competitive advantage. Value will have to be jointly created by both the firm and the consumer".[7]

At this aim it is critical to keep clear the difference between what is and what is not co-creation. For example, co-creation is not paying maximum attention to the customer needs and opinions or designing an effective or luxurious customer service, it is rather joint creation of value by the company and the customer or involving the customer in co-designing a service experience which best fits in their context.

Communities of connected, informed, empowered, and active consumers are challenging the firm-centric view of the world. Patients want to engage in dialogue. They want to understand the risk-benefits of alternative options of treatment.

The implications in terms of communication and branding are easily understood.

Building Blocks of Interactions: Dialogue, Access, Risk-Benefits, and Transparency (DART)

According to Prahalad and Ramaswamy (2004),[8] "in order to build a system for co-creation of value, we need to start with the 'building blocks of interactions'

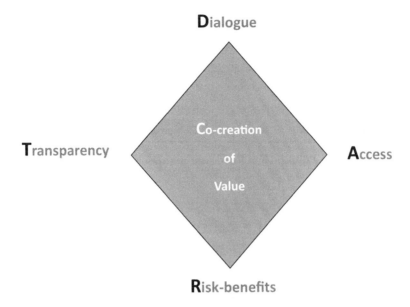

Figure 10.1   Building blocks of interactions for co-creation of value
Source: Prahalad and Ramaswamy, 2004.

Communities of connected, informed, empowered, and active consumers are challenging the firm-centric view of the world.

between the organization and consumers that facilitate co-creation experiences, that is Dialogue, Access, Risk-benefits, and Transparency (DART)" (see Figure 10.1).

- *Dialogue*: Besides motivating information sharing, it facilitates understanding between companies and customers while giving each participant a better opportunity to play an active role in the process of value creation process.

- *Access*: Enables each participant to build his/her own experience results (that is, information and on-demand resources) by providing them with knowledge, tools and expertise.

- *Risk Management*: Assumes that if consumers become co-creators of value with companies, they will demand more information about potential risks of goods and services, but they may also have to bear more responsibility for dealing with those risks: disclosure, debate the trade-off, sharing responsibility.

- *Transparency*: Transparency of information in interaction processes is necessary for individuals to participate effectively in co-creation, and generate trust between institutions and individuals: reduced opaqueness, transfer understandings (Srivastava and Verma, 2012).[9]

Dialogue, access, and transparency can lead to a clearer assessment by the consumer of the risk-benefits of an action and a related decision. Should I change my medication? What are the risks of changing? Instead of just depending on the doctor—the expert—the patient has the tools and the support structure to help make that decision—not in some generic risk category but "for me"—with a medical condition, a lifestyle, or social obligations. This is a personalized understanding of risk-benefits.

The progress towards DART cannot be stopped. The case of the patient–doctor interaction is not isolated.

The opportunities for value creation are enhanced significantly for organizations that accept the concepts of personalized co-creation experience as the source of unique value. Personalizing the co-creation experience differs from the concept of "customers as innovators."

Dialogue, access, and transparency can lead to a clearer assessment by the consumer of the risk-benefits of an action and a related decision.

Personalizing the co-creation experience means nurturing customized interactions and experience outcomes.

A personalized co-creation experience implies how individuals choose to interact with the experience environment that the firm facilitates. What Prahalad and Ramaswamy (2004) are suggesting is a totally different process—one that involves individual consumers on their terms—a broad challenge that business leaders must face.

Different Forms of Crowdsourcing

Although there are still multiple definitions of crowdsourcing, one constant has been the dissemination of problems to the public, and an open call for contributions to solving the problem. Members of the public submit solutions which are then owned by the entity which disseminates the problem. In some cases, the contributor of the solution is compensated monetarily, with prizes or with recognition. In other cases, the only rewards may be status or intellectual satisfaction. Crowdsourcing may produce solutions from amateurs or volunteers, working in their spare time, or from experts or small businesses which were unknown to the initiating organization.[10]

Crowdsourcing can have three main different forms:

- *Open innovation programs* through online platforms such as Innocentive.com and NineSights.com. Clients manage Innovation Galleries on the platform. These galleries enable the companies to post technology needs, collaborate on an ongoing basis with a global network of innovators, and drive awareness of their innovation programs.

The opportunities for value creation are enhanced significantly for organizations that accept the concepts of personalized co-creation experience as the source of unique value.

- *Grand challenges* enable organizations to uncover real solutions to the world's most pressing problems. Recent programs include: The CCEMC (Climate Change and Emissions Management Corporation) Grand Challenge to achieve a net reduction of greenhouse gases by one megatonne per year. CCEMC recently awarded CAD$12 million to 24 Round One winners. Head Health Challenges sponsored by GE, the NFL, and Under Armour to advance understanding of traumatic brain injury, improve protection and diagnostic tools, and track head impacts in real time. One challenge attracted more than 450submissions—The Cisco Security Grand Challenge to secure the Internet of Things. Winners were announced in October 2014.

- *Innovation contests* involve exclusively competent organizations and experts willing to contribute to faster and more cost-effective innovation for companies aiming at developing or improving products and services.

Communicating and Branding with Crowdsourcing and Co-Creation

A crowdsourcing or co-creation project may become an "innovative" way to engage patients and generate change while communicating a message or a brand.

Organizations who are listening and involving customers in decision-making are becoming popular and better liked by them. Leveraging the internal collaboration programs with external communication planning has an impact on the overall brand perception and/or communication expected result. This is not the main goal, but a very welcome indirect effect of a crowdsourcing competition or a co-creation project.

A crowdsourcing or co-creation project may become an "innovative" way to engage patients and generate change while communicating a message or a brand.

As anticipated above, while designing these types of programs it is crucial to focus on:

- developing the marketing campaign;

- developing and realizing events aiming at amplifying the message;

- planning an effective social media campaign.

In fact, after the identification, ideation, and design of the topic or problem to be co-created or crowdsourced, you will need to launch the competition/ project and *develop both an online and offline marketing campaign* which should include events, workshops, social media, and, eventually, advertising.

Successful crowdsourcing and co-creation programs combine a startling kick-off and the message is translated and effectively communicated to the various previously identified audiences. Since the duration of each program is usually medium/long, it is very important to plan in advance and adapt, as the program unfolds, a set of ideas, contents, and activities aiming at keeping up excitement for an extended period of time. Since each program produces a result, be it a new product/service or a solution to a problem, you will have to plan an effective communication plan to "celebrate" the "grand finale."

In addition to the marketing communication campaign, *project administration* offers a number of opportunities to relate, engage, and communicate with customers or potential customers. In fact, you will need to continue engaging participants (that is, with live demo/pitches, award ceremony/moderation/ideas/and so on) throughout the duration of the project till the grand finale.

Healthcare Organizations Using Crowdsourcing and Co-Creation to Innovatively Communicate with Their Patients and Enhance Their Experience

Besides PatientsLikeMe, some other interesting and ground-breaking healthcare organizations are already using crowdsourcing to innovatively communicate with their patients and enhance their experience:[11]

Successful crowdsourcing and co-creation programs combine a startling kick-off and the message is translated and effectively communicated to the various previously identified audiences.

- *CrowdMed* charges patients a $199 fee to share their disease experience and obtain a probable diagnosis from the crowd of MDs ("medical detectives" in this case). Almost 3,000 MDs (doctors and residents) have registered as medical detectives.

- *Webicina* is a site where medicine combines with social media to allow physicians across the world to communicate their findings easily, quickly, and effectively.

- *Biopharma company UCB* partnered with PatientsLikeMe to create an online, open epilepsy community that captures real-world experiences of people living with epilepsy in the US. Launched in early 2010, this platform is designed to collect, analyze, and reflect information received from people with epilepsy, regardless of their diagnosis, prognosis, or treatment regimen (Brodie, 2002).[12]

- *CureTogether* is a social health collaborative that brings patients with hundreds of conditions together in overlapping data communities. CureTogether was launched in July 2008 by Alexandra Carmichael and Daniel Reda to help the people they knew and the millions they didn't who live in daily chronic pain. Starting with three conditions, it quickly expanded as people wrote in to request that their conditions be added to this ongoing study. CureTogether is a social business, currently funded by its founders and angel investment, and has partnered with several universities and research organizations.[13]

- *GE partnered with Kaggle to launch crowdsourced "Quests."* The hospital quest is an open call for application ideas that will incorporate operational solutions "that can promote an improved health care system experience for patient and family." The hospital competition features a judges' panel, made up of representatives from GE, Ochsner Health System, and Kaggle. They will be evaluating ideas on their overall quality, potential impact, and ease of adoption and implementation. While medicine should be left to the professionals, many aspects of hospital operations are ripe for rethinking. In this Quest, focus on operational (non-medical) solutions that can promote an improved health care system experience for patient and family.[14]

Likewise, some interesting and ground-breaking healthcare organizations are already using co-creation to innovatively communicate with their patients and enhance their experience.

- *TickiT*. A collaborative industry and academic partnership with the Emily Carr University of Art and Design (ECUAD) conducted the co-creation process aiming at leveraging youth's comfort with technology to develop TickiT, a youth-friendly interactive mobile eHealth psychosocial screening tool. Whitehouse et al. (2013) chose to use co-creation processes and methods with the goal of increasing patient engagement and simplifying HCP work, thereby improving patient/provider communication and experience while meeting regulatory requirements. Here co-creation process differs from the traditional method of involving passive stakeholders during the latter phase of prototype testing. It, instead, views them as active contributors with knowledge and skills for co-creation during the ideation phase.[15]

- *Flamingo and Epic Pharmacy Healthcare Co-Creation Partnership.* The Flamingo platform launched in 2014 supports a new and innovative approach to customer relationships and retention. Flamingo is a leading Australian software developer while Epic Pharmacy (EPIC), is one of Australia's largest, specialty pharmacy groups providing hospital, oncology, and aged care pharmacy services. This innovative platform enables customers to co-create their desired experience by personalizing the way they communicate, how they interact with and want to be treated by an organization, and the mix of goods or services they want to receive.[16]

Think like the end healthcare consumer

Notes

1   Maibach, E.W., Abroms, L.C. and Marosits M. (2007), Communication and Marketing as Tools to Cultivate the Public's Health: A Proposed "People and Places" Framework, BMC Public Health [online] Available at http://www.biomedcentral.com/1471–2458/7/88 [Accessed 20 September 2014].

2   Deci, E.D. and Ryan, R.M. (2002), *Handbook of Self-Determination Research*. New York: University of Rochester Press.

3   Borfitz, D. (2013), PatientsLikeMe: Outcome Measures About to Get Crowdsourced, BioIT World [online]. Available at http://www.bio-itworld.com/2013/2/25/patientslikeme-outcome-measures-about-to-get-crowdsourced.html [Accessed 25 November 2014].

4   Eitel, B. (2013), PatientsLikeMe: Crowdsourcing Healthcare, Crowdsourcing—The industry website [online]. Available at http://www.crowdsourcing.org/article/patientslikeme-crowdsourcing-health-care/24209 [Accessed 25 November 2015].

5   McBride, R. (2013), PatientsLikeMe Leads Crowdsourcing for Patient Outcomes. FierceBiotechIT.

6   Prahalad, C.K. and Ramaswamy V. (2004), Co-Creation Experiences: The Next Practice in Value Creation. *Journal of Interactive Marketing*, 18(3). Published online in Wiley InterScience (www.interscience.wiley.com).

7   Prahalad, C.K. and Ramaswamy V. (2004), Co-Creation Experiences: The Next Practice in Value Creation. *Journal of Interactive Marketing*, 18(3). Published online in Wiley InterScience (www.interscience.wiley.com).

8   Prahalad, C.K. and Ramaswamy V. (2004), Co-Creation Experiences: The Next Practice in Value Creation. *Journal of Interactive Marketing*, 18(3). Published online in Wiley InterScience (www.interscience.wiley.com).

9   Srivastava, R.M. and Verma, S. (2012), *Strategic Management: Concepts, Skills and Practices*. Delhi: PHI Learning Pvt. Ltd, p. 194.

10   Howe, J. (2006), "The Rise of Crowdsourcing." *Wired*.

11   Beyond Bandwidth Level 3 Communication blog, 2013. Not Alone in a Crowd: Crowdsourcing for Healthcare. Level 3 Editor, Level 3 Communication, LLC [online]. Available at http://blog.level3.com/healthcare/not-alone-in-a-crowd-crowdsourcing-for-healthcare/ [Accessed 25 November 2014].

12   Brodie, M.J. and Kwan, P. (2002), Staged Approach to Epilepsy Management. *Neurology*, suppl. 5, p. 58.

13   CureTogether Blog, [online]. Available at http://curetogether.com/blog/about/ [Accessed 1 December 2014].

14   Root, A. (2012), Crowdsourcing.org, The industry website. GE Partners with Kaggle, Launches Crowdsourced "Quests" [online]. Available at http://www.crowdsourcing.org/editorial/ge-partners-with-kaggle-launches-crowdsourced-quests/22206 [Accessed 1 December 2014].

15   Whitehouse, S.R. et al. (2013), Co-Creation With TickiT: Designing and Evaluating a Clinical eHealth Platform for Youth. *Journal of Medical Internet Research Research Protocols*, 2(2): e42.

16   Flamingo (2014). Epic Pharmacy Injects $1.5 Million into Flamingo Healthcare Co-creation Platform [online]. Available at http://new.flamingo.io/press/epic-pharmacy-injects-1-5-million-flamingo-healthcare-co-creation-platform/ [Accessed 31 December 2014].

Index

For Product Safety Concerns and Information please contact our EU
representative GPSR@taylorandfrancis.com Taylor & Francis Verlag GmbH,
Kaufingerstraße 24, 80331 München, Germany

Printed and bound by CPI Group (UK) Ltd, Croydon, CR0 4YY

01/05/2025

01858363-0002